Heroin is the Answer

A memoir of what I can remember

Heroin is the Answer

A memoir of what I can remember

By

Russell Holbrook

Splatterpiece Press
Mableton, GA

Copyright © 2019 by Russell Holbrook

All rights reserved
Printed in the United States of America

A note to readers:
I have only used the names of individuals by whom I was given the express permission to do so, and to those brave and generous souls, I give my deepest love and thanks.

Published by
Splatterpiece Press
5277 Maple Valley Rd. SW
Mableton, GA
30126

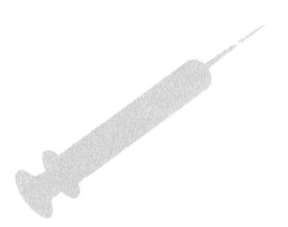

Heroin is the Answer:
A Memoir of What I Can Remember
Splatterpiece Press #002
ISBN: 9781796286311

No Part of this book may be reproduced, stored in a retrieval system, or transmitted in any form or by any means, including mechanical, electric, photocopying, recording, or otherwise, without the prior written permission of the publisher or author.

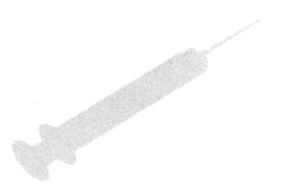

Also by Russell Holbrook

JOY
(Riot Forge)

Crust
(New Kink Books)

Lucy Furr
(Splatterpiece Press)

For Betty Ann and Parker

"Be a good boy, go get fucked up."
— J. McClain

The Beginning of the Beginning: A Forward

When I grow up or when I grow old - whichever may come first- who knows what in the good fuck I will remember. Maybe I'll draw blanks every time I strain to recall these days or maybe everything will teeter and tumble out and I'll paint vivid pictures with recollection, and beautiful memories will fill pages and I'll have a book. But I'm afraid that wouldn't happen, so I've decided to write it all down now. Fuck the future –this may be the only time I've got. With every cigarette I smoke time slips and I'm thinking, "I really want to do something worthwhile." A small contribution to our beautiful, useless human race, my part in the play, it's a speaking part but I'm not sure who's writing my lines. I used to believe it was me, but now who knows?

Tonight, all my friends are visiting with a certain boy. He is the opiate of lackadaisical sweetness. When you're with him life is so incredible, and every little detail carries an incomprehensible magnitude. On my visits with him, I've often asked myself where this great concern and affection for life comes from, and why I had not noticed this beauty before. It's like instant childhood in a spoon. However, heroin is most comparable to the sweetest memories of life; the feeling I get when I have the greatest nostalgia and fade out into the past. A warm feeling fills me, coming up from my stomach to my eyes, and a smile curves my lips. I'm high. Heroin is everything beautiful and nice and comfortable coming through a pinhole subway and into my blood. Fuck it, I'm high.

```
Diary
Fall, 1997
```

Part I

A Costume of 100 Cool Corners

Untitled (#1)

It's time to write a new book

The forward is finished, now the story begins.

I'm going to peel back space: layers of shooting stars, a bracing comfort.

Dear, empathetic reader, please believe in light

And watch the waking moon fade behind your eyes.

Winter, 1997

OnE (fall, 1997)

The day he came into the world I showed up at the hospital a little after six a.m.: late, alone, and the last to arrive. The night before his birth, I hadn't been at home with his mom helping her prepare for the big day. I was at Six Flags with a friend, tripping on acid, high on painkillers, riding roller coasters and denying all reality, feeling worthless and ruined yet still trying to cope in the only way I knew how.

This is my last night of freedom, I'd told myself. *After this one last night I'll straighten out, I'll be good, I'll become responsible, I'll do the right thing, I'll be a dad, for real, I will. I promise.*

But then there was the harsh pain of the following day where vows and promises fade into the brittle morning light.

After a quick cigarette, I walked up the hill from the pavillion to the front doors. I stepped under the front awning. The sliding glass doors closed in front of me.

"You're not getting past me," the doors said in a stern, robotic tone. My face crumpled.

"But, I have to," I said.

"Why? No one wants you in there, you stupid, worthless fuck. You weren't there for her during the pregnancy, what makes you think you have any right to be here now?"

The words of the doors stung my ears and my heart. I felt like they were right, but, I still had to go in. I hung my head and stared at the carpet mat beneath my feet. "It's the right thing to do. I need to be here."

The door laughed in a deep baritone, it's doors sliding back and forth with each guffaw. I felt tears brimming in the corners of my eyes. I shouted. "Stop laughing at me!" I looked up.

A nurse was wheeling an elderly man out the front door. I smiled in embarassment and slinked through the open entrance.

As the morning dragged on, we discovered that Parker wasn't coming out the usual way. When they wheeled his mom away to cut him out, I went to hide in my car, tucked away somewhere in a corner of the parking deck, telling myself that I would go back in when the operation was over. Once nestled into the safety of my car, I cranked up the heat, covered myself in a homemade quilt my grandmother had given me and hit play on side two of the Tori Amos cassette I'd lifted from my sister's tape collection. I curled up in the front seat, closed my eyes, and shivered, wishing I had more dope to put in my veins. It was mid-morning, maybe about six or eight hours since I'd shot up a spoonful of heroin after my friend Garret and I had arrived home from Six Flags, and my skin felt like it was about to peel.

      I pulled the quilt closer, but it couldn't get close enough. It still wore the comforting fragrance of the old closet at my grandmother's house, where it had likely languished for years before it somehow came into my possession. I always kept it in my car because you never know when a good quilt will come in handy. Sometimes a quilt can make everything better; but not that day. It couldn't cover up all the fear or regret or pain or hate or shame I felt. It couldn't cover the hollow crater in my soul. And it couldn't keep out the cold that steadily crept over my body, spreading along on the inside my skin.

Untitled (#2)

Will I hear my son's voice over the warm rush in my ears?

Go downtown in a heap to find our sweet lady on the street

Supply and demand

I find what I don't need

Then —fade up, into night

Driving until the tank is dry

God whispers in my ear

But speaks a foreign language I once studied but fucking forgot to write down

Remember the feelings

Fade out and away

With the world on my knees in a child's smile,

Burping up innocence and gurgling out pain

Fall, 1997

TWho (Back-up: Summer, 1997)

The first time heroin flowed through my veins, I didn't inject it myself. I let this guy who I didn't know and whose name I can't recall, but who seemed nice enough and had a needle all full and ready, put it into my body for me. This guy was a friend of Hadley's and I was sure he was alright so there was nothing to worry about, right? And Hadley was alright -I'd known her for a day and a half and I was sure she was a wonderful and trustworthy person because you can always trust a pretty girl who does drugs.

I'd met Hadley the night before at a party my friend Janie was throwing at The Shack. I wasn't sleeping with Janie anymore. I wasn't sleeping with anyone. I was single and sitting on the tattered, lime green couch by myself, maybe drinking or smoking a cigarette, when I looked up and saw Hadley smiling, looking at me from across the shack's main room. The shack was a small guest house next to Janie's house. That was where everyone partied, and if you considered getting blanked out of your mind on whatever substance was available and possibly falling down stairs or stumbling into the swimming pool in the dark to be a good time, then you were in the right place.

I think I got up and walked over to Hadley or maybe she sat down next to me but somehow; we ended up talking and by the end of the night I was out on the driveway with her and her two closest girlfriends, making plans for the immediate future. Our conversation had turned to our collective favorite subject- drugs- and a certain drug in particular. These three girls knew about heroin. They'd *done* it. They knew where to get it. And yes, they could get me some.

I felt a rush of excitement come over me. Rainbows sprouted from my eyes and everything became bright and wonderful. Finding out where to get heroin was exactly what I'd been hoping for. Pretty girls really can make all your dreams come true.

Cut to the next night. We were in Hadley's driveway, crowded into a two-door car. That very nice and agreeable guy I already mentioned was pushing a loaded needle into my arm, which was what I'd wanted ever since I'd decided that my life was over, which was because of a few things.

The band I loved more than breathing, that I'd been playing in and devoting myself to for the previous five years, had broken up. I'd lost my record deal, I had dropped out of college, I couldn't make it through a waking day without being loaded, and then -to make things just that much more fun and interesting- I'd learned I had created another human being and now that new human would need my help to make his way in the world, the fucking shitty, depressing, disappointing, deplorable world. It was too much -all of it- I couldn't handle it.

I'd decided that life as I'd known it was over and done, and I was at peace with my decision. All I needed was a way out. But since I wasn't one to rush into things like suicide, I wanted a slow destruction device; I needed to take my time, just so I could be sure.

The nice guy pulled back the needle's plunger. The chamber clouded with blood. "Always make sure you see blood so you'll know you hit the vein," he said.

He pushed in the plunger and it all became real. God leaned in close and gave me a hug. The universe cheered and smiled. Angels and crickets sang together in the yard, and on that idyllic summer night, a miracle happened. In an instant, heroin washed away all the pain, hate, guilt, and shame. I knew I had found the answer, and a smile lit up my face.

Untitled (#3)

I was always holding what weighed too much

To drop on my feet when my fingers turned white

Balancing on one foot for a lifetime

With one arm, propping myself up on an innocent bystander

I would share my thoughts, but I don't speak your language

Breathe in the beauty

The purest flow of thought, rhyme, and meter

Summer, 1997

Three (fall, 1997)

When I told my dad he had just become a grandfather, his reaction was: a. understated; b. unremarkable; or, c. I was so high I had no hope of interpreting his reaction in any logical or meaningful way.

I'd come home that night with a Polaroid of myself cradling my brand-new son in my arms. I went straight to my sister's place. She was living with her boyfriend in the guesthouse across the driveway from our parents' house. I was staying in my parents' house, the same room I spent my high school years in, which is where I'd landed when I'd left college.

I showed the photo to everyone who was there: my sister, her boyfriend, and whoever else may have been hanging out that night -there always seemed to be people hanging out there. They cheered and offered hugs and congratulations, and their warm reception made me feel better for a minute. I think I almost felt normal. Then, someone decided that we needed to commemorate the joyous occasion.

Grab your needles and your spoons! A celebration is in order! Russell is a dad! Russell is a dad!

Burning confetti rained down from the ceiling. An abbreviated parade of armless amputee clowns rode through the living room on unicycles, belting out the chorus to "Beautiful Boy (Darling Boy)". Someone passed me a clean spoon and a new needle. I took a seat on the floor.

Approximately maybe twelve minutes and two bags of dope later, my mind was swimming in a pool of blissful nothingness, my body was warm and cozy, and I felt that everything would be okay. Everything *was* okay. And since everything was okay, it was safe for me to go tell my dad -he of the Baptist religion and the no babies outside of marriage and the pride in the family name- the happy news. He wouldn't be able to hurt or kill me since I had put my heroin armor on.

I guess he didn't take the news well, but then again, my memory of that night is spotty. I remember handing him the Polaroid. His hand seemed to shake as if struggling under the weight of the photograph and the reality it brought with it. I was almost sure I could hear him thinking as he walked out onto the back porch in silence and lit up a Doral 100: *Not only is my adult son -who I tried my best to raise upright- a ne'er-do-well college drop-out loser musician fuckhead, but now he's given me an illegitimate grandchild. Well, goddamnit isn't that just wonderful!*

But dad said nothing. The silence was pure fucking agonizing torture. If he did say anything that night, I can't remember what it was. My one memory is the image of him standing at the edge of the back porch, in front of the pool, tugging on his cigarette, plumes of smoke rising into the air, his back toward me as he stared out into the darkness, probably thinking some angry or depressing shit.

I wonder if he knew I was wasted. I wonder if he knew how wasted I was. I wonder if I puked that night. Probably, I usually did.

Dad must have told mom, or maybe I did, even though I'm sure I didn't want to. There was the toxic cloud of shame that surrounded having a kid out of wedded bliss and I was already feeling it choking me, so, I probably didn't tell her. A day or so after I told my dad my mom found me in my room and told me in her stern yet quiet way we were going to the hospital because she wanted to see her grandchild. If my mom ever cursed, I'm sure this would have been an ideal time. Instead, her words were short and concise, terse and painful, full of hurt and confusion. The birth of her first grandbaby, what could have been a cheerful occasion she surely would have wanted to be present for, was instead something she found out about after the fact, from someone who found out about it from his very inebriated son. What kind of person doesn't tell their mom she will be a grandmother? Answer: Someone scared shitless of being a disappointment and a fuck-up and a failure; someone who is so horrified of these possible fates he fulfills them all in surplus; someone who was me.

The next thing I remember is being in an elevator, the fluorescent lights stabbing my eyes with their tiny white daggers, attacking my brain with their incessant hum, laughing and mocking my misery. My mother was scowling. The pulleys and cables and the motor whirred behind the elevator walls, seeming so loud that I could feel them inside my skull. The numbers lit up as we ascended to the maternity ward. The elevator came to a stop, there was a ding, the doors slid open, and we stepped out into the hallway, greeted by the sterile aroma of freshly mopped floors wafting through the air. I thought I could hear all the babies in the ward, squirming out of their swaddling clothes, leaving their rooms, the patter of little feet echoing through the corridor. Then I saw them, coming toward me brandishing scalpels, bone saws, and other instruments of surgical demise. Their eyes were black and full of hate; they held their weapons high as they wobbled toward me on chubby legs, dragging their umbilical cords behind them. "Look what you did to us!" They screamed. "You brought us here and left us all alone; and now you will pay!"

My breath hitched in my throat. A nurse smiled and walked by. I blinked and saw my mother standing next to me. I exhaled and swallowed hard and we began the seemingly endless walk down the hall.

I was cold. My skin was crawling. Everything felt harsh and scary. I wanted to be back on a couch somewhere, a space heater warming my feet and an Enya CD playing on repeat while I pushed drugs into my veins. I sniffled. We stopped at the door. This was it: Betty Ann's room. I cringed and shuffled inside.

Untitled (#4)

This is true separation

Somewhere someone drew a line, but no one told me

They yelled "Dance!" and nailed my feet to the floor

They put my arms in slings and broke my wrists

That day my heart grew ten sizes but was still too small

Small beams of light struggle through tangled arms

Hit us in the eyes, in that special corner where it glistens and glows

Only to be crushed when the arm is amputated

No arm = No dream

I want to feel the cool deep swell around my body

Skid me away into nothing and being –numb

A shell.   **Fall, 1997**

Fo4Ur (fall, 1997)

The memory of my mom holding Parker is cloudy and dim. I don't remember if she smiled, but she probably did because she usually does. I remember a nurse or someone, handing me papers and telling me I needed to sign them. They were the records of live birth.

I stalled. I protested in silence. I didn't want to sign. It terrified me. The type-set words that covered the pages formed a malevolent grin. "Sign us," the papers said. "Give us your life; you have no choice."

I heard hundreds of versions of my voice screaming inside my head. *I can't have a kid -I'm still a kid! I'm a total fuck-up! I don't want this! I can't do this! I'll ruin this little baby's life! His mom hates me! Everyone hates me! Please, someone, get me the fuck out of here!*

My heart raced. I struggled to appear calm and not twitch in my chair. I felt like the still air in the room was trying to suffocate me.

My mom looked at me, into me, and through me, her expression unyielding as she told me to sign. Seeing far into her steely, determined eyes, I felt a childlike fear overtake me. My hand trembled, and I felt sick as I moved the pen over the paper. And then there it was: my signature on official legal documents. I was somebody's dad. It was real. Holy shit oh my fucking God I'm gonna puke it was real.

Time skipped like a scratch on an overplayed LP and my mom and I were leaving. There were no smiles, only sad glances and my mother's jaw set somewhere between heartbreak and fury. I mostly stared at the floor and thought about how much I hated myself and how worthless and useless I was. And I wondered what I would do. Then it came, and the answer was so obvious. I would get high and forget all about this and then I could figure things out and move on with my life. After realizing that, I felt better. It was good to have a plan.

Untitled (#5)

Surrounded by misery

                 "It's fucking trying to pull loose every bone in my body"

Pressing me into shapes and boxes

Suffocating

The life snatchers

Search for nothing with broken hands

  Senseless <u>useless</u> circle of life

Circling in place

  Never changing

  Never ending

  Always Dying

Fall, 1997

Fiiiive (fall 1994—spring 1995: A Backstory)

I'd met Betty Ann near the end of the fall quarter of my freshman year at college. I was living in Macon, Ga, attending Mercer University, sort of studying art and philosophy but mostly learning about the important things in life, like sex, drugs, and rock-and-roll, and having important experiences like stealing MXPX and Starflyer 59 cassettes from the Christian bookstore at the local mall and chugging bottles of cough syrup because I thought we were going to see *Natural Born Killers* but instead my friends and I end up playing hacky sack in the parking lot of a truck stop strip club somewhere near Warner Robins while our other friends are inside sticking crumbled bills into the thongs of strippers dancing on a stage covered with dirty carpet, distant stares in their eyes, with the glare of fluorescent lights beaming down on their shiny, freshly washed hair.

During that first quarter, I came home pretty much every weekend. Apparently, Betty Ann had spotted me at one of the punk shows we both frequented at the Somber Reptile, Atlanta's greatest dive club ever, at least for my generation. A friend of Betty Ann's told me that Betty Ann liked me. I didn't know who Betty Ann was, but I wanted to, and because the thought of a girl liking me and the possibility of what that could lead to was exciting, I got her number from the aforementioned friend, and when I came home to stay for the extended Christmas break, I summoned my courage and dialed Betty Ann's number.

I totally remember that call. Her voice drifted over the line tender and sweet. She said she had just gotten out of the bath. My mind swam with images of water dripping off her wet hair, splashing on her bare shoulders, her body wrapped tight in a thin towel that hugged all her curves in just the right places. I felt heat flush across my stomach. My heart beat with a sincere purpose. I liked her voice. I liked the things she said. I liked *her*.

We talked for a while, but I don't know how long. I asked her if she would like to hang out soon. She said she would. I smiled electric when I hung up the phone.

I wish I had every memory clear and shining and ready for retrieval. I don't remember where we were the first time I saw her face to face, the first time we touched, or our first kiss. But I remember the first time we said the words - *those words*- the special, sometimes terrifying, always irretrievable words that change everything.

We had been hanging out at her house. The street sat dark and quiet and I was at my car about to leave, my heart warm and my soul singing, when I heard her front door open. I looked up to see her dart out of the house. She hurried across the lawn and caught me as I was unlocking my door.

She grabbed onto me.

"I love you," she said, her eyes wide and full.

My heart swelled and flipped sideways. I felt something beyond joy I can't quite describe, but it's like feeling everything and nothing all at once, like being washed away in a perfect oblivion.

I could have stammered or hesitated, but I didn't. It was such a gorgeous and natural moment that the words just flowed out of me as if I'd been waiting to say them my entire life.

"I love you too," I said.

She beamed a smile at me that says those things we don't know how to say, and then she ran back inside, grabbing my heart and taking it with her.

It seems like Betty Ann and I spent every night and most days and afternoons together during Christmas break. I remember the taste of her kisses. I remember the warmth and softness of her lips. I remember the smell of her skin. I remember so much that I wish I could remember it all.

Christmas break of freshman year was the best Christmas break, ever. Then, as soon as it had begun, it ended, and I was on my way back to school. I hated to leave her, but I did my best to stay positive. Once I was back at school, Betty Ann and I talked on the phone, saw each other whenever we could, and tried to stay close to each other. The winter dragged on, and after some time, the end came into view; first, just a dim dot on the horizon, then growing closer and clearer with each passing day.

One day in March or maybe April 1995, I drove up to Atlanta to meet Betty Ann at the mall. For the past couple of weeks, I'd been sensing that something was wrong. I practically knew it when I saw her that day.

With sad eyes, she said she was breaking up with me. I felt my chest collapse. I didn't understand. She couldn't explain, or she wouldn't. Didn't she love me? She said she loved me too much. What the fuck did that mean? Couldn't we fix it? No, there would be no fixing. It was over. I couldn't believe it. We'd broken up, and that was that.

Maybe she said she was sorry, maybe I said I was sorry too. I remember walking away crushed, feeling like I was wearing iron shoes.

I hung my head, staring at the floor as I plodded to the other side of the mall to some restaurant I can't remember the name of. I was meeting my college buddy Thaddeus there, so we could work on our papers before we drove back to Macon. I told him what had happened. He offered me his condolences along with a cigarette. I accepted both.

I probably smoked at least a half a pack of Luckies and drank about twelve cups of coffee that afternoon. I did my best to focus on my schoolwork, but the pain of my freshly eviscerated heart kept creeping back to the surface. I lit another smoke and tried to turn off my feelings.

Thaddeus and I worked on our papers until closing time, which worked out well because we were almost out of smokes. As we were leaving, Thad had to visit the restroom or something, so we agreed to meet back at the car. Once alone, my thoughts turned back to Betty Ann. I hooked my thumbs under the straps of my backpack and headed for the nearest exit. I didn't even know which exit I was going to, I just wanted to be outside, out of that fucking building. I came around an escalator and there was Betty Ann, sitting on a bench next to some guy. My body went numb and my breath grew short. I didn't even know who the dude was, and I never found out, I just know he wasn't me. I walked faster as I passed them. I looked at her; she looked away.

It felt so wrong, to hurry past the person I loved more than anyone in the world, the woman I'd lost my spiritual virginity to, the girl I'd told my best friend I wanted to marry, to walk by without a word, our eyes never meeting, as if we didn't know each other at all.

My heart was so hurt that it got so mad at me it tore itself out of my chest and jumped down to the floor. "You idiot!" My heart screamed at me, "How could you let that girl hurt me like this?!" My heart pointed to a gaping wound in the center of his body that squirted blood onto the shiny mall floor every time he breathed.

  I protested. "But I didn't do anything! I don't understand what happened!"

  My heart screamed in agony, turned gray, and fell over. It hit the floor and disintegrated into a pile of ash. A janitor walked up and swept my heart into a dustpan and dumped it in his rolling garbage can. He looked at me and shook his head. "Stupid kid…" he mumbled as he walked away.

  I kept walking and hoped that I wouldn't cry.

  A gust of temperate spring air washed over me when I pushed out of the exit. I breathed in deep. When I got to the car Thaddeus was leaning up against the passenger side door, smoking, looking like he couldn't give a fuck and looking cool doing it. *He's so rock 'n' roll,* I thought. He nodded at me and exhaled a cloud of smoke. The breeze tossed his long dark hair against the side of his face. I may have smiled, or at least smirked. He asked if I was ready to go. I replied that *hell yes*, I was.

We hopped in the car and took off, leaving the mall and jumping on 75 south. Thad cranked up Sebadoh on the stereo. Lou Barlow crooning about the pain of young love was like balm on my spirit. I fired up a Lucky and took it all in. The clouds parted overhead, and sunshine poured into our hearts as we raced back to school on that late Sunday afternoon.

Untitled (#6)

SHE was everywhere I went

Until her eyes closed and we both stopped bothering to care

Thinking it would be okay was just a dream

Writing words to a song I would never sing

Spring, 1995

6SiiXXX (spring, 1995)

My first real drink, followed quickly by my first real succession of drinks, was at a Christmas party during my senior year of high school. It was gin. I thought its taste resembled the smell of wood floor cleaner. It made my face twist into knots and I chased it with soda. I took that drink with the expressed intention of getting drunk, and that was an intention which stayed with me until I could finally get sober for good some nineteen years later.

After Betty Ann and I broke up, I seemed to notice –really notice- the liquor bottles that filled the bottom drawer of my college roommate's chest of drawers for the first time. They were so pretty and shiny. I asked them what they were doing down there in the drawer. They said they were there to help me feel better. I thanked them and accepted their help with a glad heart although I never told them I preferred the help of Marijuana at the time; I didn't want to hurt their feelings.

I don't remember how much of Nate's vodka and rum and whatever else I drank. I remember going to the infirmary once with a hangover that was so painful it scared me. I don't remember if Nate knew I was drinking his booze; he never mentioned it.

One morning near sunrise, after being up all night drinking and getting high on something, maybe weed or acid or probably both, I ended up in a public park somewhere in downtown Macon, having a heart-to-heart with a homeless man. Or maybe he was just an early riser and liked wearing dirty clothes and hanging out in the gazebo? Whatever the case, he was kind, and to my young mind, magical and wise. After regaling the old man with my tale of heartbreak, and how much I missed Betty Ann, and how I wasn't sure if I'd ever be okay again, a sincere look of sympathy fell over his face and he gave me a knowing smile. He also may have been thinking how young and stupid I was. Whatever thoughts may or may not have been in his mind, he told me I was young, I had my health, and that there was nothing to worry about because I was like "a kid in a candy store". He followed that statement with something obscene, wherein he made liberal use of many colorful words to describe female anatomy, and then he continued on to tell me that Betty Ann dumping me was not, in fact, the end life as I knew it and that, eventually, everything would be all right. Then he scratched his balls, spit, and asked me for a cigarette. We each smoked a Lucky and then, after thanking him for his comforting conversation, I left the gazebo.

I wandered farther into the city and ended up in the sanctuary of a Catholic church, observing mass. Since my parents raised me Baptist, I thought the cathedral was strange, exotic, and creepy in a dark romantic way. The atmosphere filled me with reverence and I felt my spirit move. Unexpectedly, I stayed for the entire mass. After the service, I walked uphill. I knew I was heading toward my school, but I still didn't know quite where I was. My stomach rumbled, and I walked into a soul food diner that seemed to have materialized out of my need for food. Like magic, it was just there. I shuffled in and took a seat at the counter.

I sat at the counter, sipping hot coffee, feeling wonderfully out of place. I was so excited to be experiencing real culture in the real Macon, away from fake-ass school. I didn't realize I was just having breakfast with regular people on their way to work or some other everyday activity; in my mind I was having a deeply meaningful, spiritual encounter with the people of the town I lived in. I felt enamored with everyone who surrounded me.

Besides biscuits, I don't remember what I ate, but I was grateful for it and I said "Yes, Ma'am" and "Thank you" every time the kind woman behind the counter asked me if I needed more coffee or if everything was alright. Afterwards, I always remembered that magical breakfast in that wonderful little restaurant, and whenever I drove past it with friends, I would exclaim, "There it is! I love that place!" and make them listen to my tale of the enchanted breakfast experience.

Eventually, whatever I was drunk and high on that morning wore off and I knew I needed to get back to campus. I trudged along the sidewalks, the mundane misery of coming down creeping in with every step, until I found my way back to the university. I think my feet hurt. I probably skipped class and slept all day. I don't remember, but the biscuits I had that morning were totally delicious.

More days flew by. Freshman year was winding down. I was playing guitar in a band called Joe Christmas. We'd been together since 10th grade and we'd just recorded our first full-length album that February. Since then, we'd signed to a fledgling indie label out of Seattle called Tooth and Nail Records. They were planning to release our record that coming summer. Things were really starting to roll. We were playing more shows, and we were practicing more than ever before, which still wasn't all that much. One Sunday afternoon following practice, I was drunk and sitting in my car, waiting for our bass player, Ryan, to come out and drive the two of us back to Mableton. Phillip, our drummer, came down to the car. Leaning into the window, he asked me if I was okay. I told him I was fine while I wondered to myself why he was asking and why he looked so concerned. Were we about to have a heart-to-heart talk? Was he upset that I'd been pilfering from his parent's liquor cabinet the whole time we practiced that day? Phillip said he'd noticed that I'd seemed depressed over the last couple of months and that I'd been drinking a lot, like, a whole fucking lot, and not just at night, which may have been acceptable, but pretty much all the time.

I felt surprised. It worried him? I was drinking a lot? Like, a whole fucking lot... for real? I knew I felt horrible, and that I was using the booze to ease the pain of my break-up with Betty Ann, but I hadn't noticed this behavior as being anything out of the ordinary, and the person he spent the next couple of minutes describing didn't sound like me at all, or, at least that wasn't the person I'd been seeing. On the way home, I pondered the things Phillip had said. He was my good friend and if my drinking concerned him, then I thought I should probably take it to heart. The guys in our band were my best friends, so I knew he was looking out for me. With that in mind, I decided that it would be better to smoke more weed and drink less, since weed was the safer option, and then, hopefully, that would help curb my drinking too. But, even though I did go on to drink a little less and smoke a lot more, nothing really changed; I stayed depressed, I couldn't shake it. I kept medicating myself however I could just to feel better and make it through each day. And that didn't work. I knew I was sad because of the break-up, but there was something else going on that I didn't recognize, and all the while that extra thing grew and grew and got stronger, waiting to reveal itself, knowing that when the time came for it to jump out and destroy me, there might be nothing I could do to stop it.

Untitled (#7)

I can see all things

In nice arrangements, in their own small spaces

Pacing lights

Their hands in pockets

All this and that and no one and nothing,

Flowing through

In my mind, I see all things

Understanding escapes, replaced by wonder

Floating away in waves, in parts of parts

Fleeting, breaking off from the central being

Higher, higher, bringing me off the carpet

I float in small pieces of space

The train stops and I'm already on

Spring, 1995

$777eVeN (summer, 1995)

The summer of 1995 was beautiful and wonderful and all the other adjectives that can describe a halcyon time in a person's existence. It was the only period of my young adult life where I can remember being truly joyful and carefree. My family and I went on a trip to Europe that summer. We spent a week on the coast of Spain and another week in Madrid, with a day trip to Africa in between. We saw the cathedrals and toured the countryside with a talkative taxi driver. My sister and I got drunk at a café in downtown Madrid and went to see some Hollywood film that had been dubbed in Spanish. The next day she and I went to see The Cure play at the Plaza de Toros de Las Ventas, where we smoked hash with some locals, got caught in a mosh pit during Faith No More's set, and I lost my wallet. We rode the subway and somehow got back to our hostel by 2 a.m. With love for the people of that amazing continent forever imprinted on my heart, we flew back home a few days later.

Before my family trip to Europe, Joe Christmas played the Cornerstone music festival for the first time. Cornerstone was a Christian music festival that Zach, Ryan, and I had been going to almost every year since the summer after 9th grade; it was also where I got high on weed for the first time during the summer after 12th grade. Our first album -*Upstairs, Overlooking*- had come out that June, and playing at the fest in one of those huge tents in front of so many people was an incredible experience. A few of our friends from back home were the fest, too. It was so cool having them there with us, sitting up on stage, nodding along to our little songs. I remember hoping that they were proud of us, since they'd seen us play in basements for like five people, and there we were playing in front of a thousand. Later that weekend, a guy from our record label told us we would be stars in no time. I remember taking that to heart, believing it wholly and completely. *Wow, we're gonna be rock stars!* I thought to myself, grinning maniacally. Maybe he only meant that we would be rock stars in the insular, Christian music scene sense of the term, but still, we were gonna be stars! That meant that I wouldn't have to go back to college or work shitty jobs, and that I could spend all my time making music and being creative, and that (best of all!) I would be really, really, truly and totally, happy. Life was finally going to be awesome! I could not wait!

After Cornerstone and Spain, I spent the rest of the summer in a haze of drugs, booze, and music. As the summer careened into fall, I did more and more and more drugs. The winds became cold, the days darkened, and my mind grew dark as well.

Untitled (#8)

The sweetest song sings from your eyes

I know you'd say it's true

Melt into a silent daydream

Was this a decision that I was making?

Fall, 1995

Ei888ght

(Fall/winter, 1995)

When the golden summer of 1995 said goodbye and fall's humid southern winds blew in, school started up without me. I wasn't going back; I'd quit school, or at least taken a year off, to "work on the band". And by work on the band I mean, hang out on my parents' back porch smoking weed with my sister, smoking weed in our friend Tim's basement while getting educated on the classic Black Sabbath catalog, hanging out in Athens smoking weed and eating pills and drinking while listening to indie rock records, working the shittiest and most low-level part-time jobs I could find, and waiting for the record label to make our band world famous because I thought that was what record labels did. Every day I woke up and expected things to be different while every day I did the same shit over and over and over again, all the while wondering why we weren't on a tour, or why we weren't huge yet, or why I was high as fuck on my parent's back porch, alone, while everyone else was at work or school or engaged in some productive pursuit. I told myself to be patient: success would come. I took another hit off the bowl, stared off into space, and dreamed of my impending happiness and fame.

Untitled Tour Poem (#9)

This is something more than taking chances.

Spread out on a long highway to the song players

Roaming through the dark to the dawn – the mystery of the road

The wind is so much greater in the smoky clouds

One hundred and one miles to the end of my tongue

A bear can break trees, but can she topple the new earth?

There –a little raccoon living in the swamp, listening to Black Sabbath,

Getting high on sweet yellow frogs

The devil dog from hell, red-eyed baby eater

He's got swords in his back seat and he wants to kick my ass

Spring, 1996

NINE999

(Spring/summer/fall, 1996)

And then it was time to make another record. So, in April 1996, we packed all our gear, three-quarters of an ounce of weed (I'd already smoked the first quarter), hopes, and dreams into the Joe Christmas Econoline tour van and headed to Chicago to record our second album at our dream studio, Electrical Audio. Eleven hazy days later our second album was complete.

After we'd made our second record, we meandered out of the city and went on a nationwide tour that took us all the way to Ypsilanti, Michigan (where I tripped on shrooms and smoked some insanely bright green weed) to Vancouver B.C. (where I couldn't find any weed so instead drank super yummy beer and ate ketchup chips) to Hollywood (where there was lots of weed), to Orange County (where there was a lot more beer) and back home again.

After spending the summer living my dream of rocking out on tour had passed, I was back on my parents' back porch, toking on a joint alone, wondering why I was so unfortunate as to have to get a day job. Why wasn't I famous yet? Why did we have to come home? Why didn't someone book us another tour while we were on the first one? Why didn't I think to ask about that? What the fuck? This sucked -working and trying and all that shit- so I decided I needed to go back to college, because "working on the band", although it had many beautiful and awesome moments, wasn't easy and fun in the absolute, permanent vacation way I'd expected it to be. There was still this stupid huge hole in my spirit that was sore and aching every day and the band didn't fix that like I thought it would. Some days I would stand in front of the mirror, staring into the hole and its infinite darkness, watching it oozing blood and pus, wondering why nothing I put in it could patch it up. Most of the time, though, I would just cover it up with an oversized shirt. It was pretty easy to hide.

Once tour and summer were over, I decided that going back to school would solve my problems. So, in September 1996, I was back at Mercer University, hoping that this would somehow make me feel better and give my life purpose and direction and things would finally make sense. But, before any of that could happen, I had to find some weed.

Untitled (#10)

I am in a constant state of being constant:

> I can't think
>
> I can't move
>
> Heaven can't talk to me,
>
> It can't move me anymore
>
> This needs to stop,
>
> This writing sucks
>
> I just keep getting high

Fall, 1996

One-Oh₁₀ (Fall/winter, 1996)

It happens to every addict or alcoholic at some point: the flick of the switch -when using and drinking goes from being fun to being necessary. I suppose that looking back, maybe we can remember when the change came, when the whole "normal" world felt like an alien planet, and when the only time peace came was in a wave of obliteration. Maybe we can remember.

And there I was, back at school, not knowing even then I had a chemical imbalance in my brain, not believing I was a burgeoning alcoholic drug addict, just thinking I was lazy and depressed. But, I had the band, and I loved it so, so much, and I held onto it with the take-it-for-granted-like-it-will-always-be-there ambivalence that only a true slacker can achieve.

Almost every weekend, I went to Athens for practice, a show or, on special occasions, a recording session. Zach and Phillip – our respective singer/guitar strummer and drum beater extraordinaire- lived together in a leaning, creaky old house. We practiced in the big open room in the middle of their home. That house was where I spent tons of my time during that fall quarter. If I wasn't in Athens, I was out in the real Macon, at a condemned house that my friend Thaddeus shared with an elderly blues musician. Sitting on the floor in the house's one structurally sound room, I listened to blues and jazz records, smoked weed and cigarettes, and tried not to want to die.

      I half-heartedly shuffled through fall quarter until I left school again that December with a 2.0 GPA and a heavy rope of failure and shame around my neck. This time the rope was heavier than ever before. I told myself that I might return one day, and if not to Mercer, then I'd finish my art degree at another college, but deep down, I knew I had no ambitions of the sort and that my one and only priority was to stop the growing pain that nagged at my soul.

      As I moved back into my old high school room in my parents' house, *again*, I hoped and prayed that this was only another temporary setback and that sooner or later I could (hopefully) get my shit, and my life, together at last. All my friends were doing it, so why couldn't I?

Part II

The Night is where we live

Untitled (#11)

Shoot a paper bullet into my head

    From a paper cut-out gun

    I grin as I writhe

    I smile as I die

    How fucked up do I have to get

    To scrape out the insides

    Pumpkin shell,

    Dead but still trying to give what you take

    I grin while I die from the cut-out hole in my head

    The paper cut-out, pouring red crayon murder

    From the cut-out hole in my hollow paper head

```
10-9-1996
Macon, GA
```

11eleven (winter, 1997)

Back at home, I stuck to a strict and highly productive regimen. Every day I slept until at least 11 a.m. After reluctantly opening my eyes, I would crawl out of bed and head to the back porch where I spent at least two hours preparing for my day. This entailed chain smoking weed and cigarettes, drinking multiple cups of coffee and listening to my favorite depressing indie rock albums -like *Gold* by Starflyer 59. I always made time to stare off into space and daydream about what I wanted to be doing - instead of doing it- while I waited patiently for the weekend so I could go to Athens for band practice, or, even better, play a show.

Eventually, the weekend would arrive, and I'd escape my routine of impaired drudgery and depression. It was on one of those trips to Athens in January 1997 that I saw her again. It was a Friday. We were playing the 40-Watt club that night.

Zach had told me he'd seen her around town the week prior, so he'd invited her to the show. With excitement pulsing through me and my palm sweating beneath the receiver of my rotary dial phone, I told Zach that I didn't know Betty Ann was living in Athens. He said he hadn't known either, but that she'd said she would come to the show. I mumbled something else, and we talked about the show or the set list and when I'd be coming into town or whatever and no I wasn't bringing anyone with me this time and in the back of my mind, the whole time I was thinking *oh my God, oh my God, oh my God she will be there holy fuck oh my god!* A voice popped into my head and told me she might not show and that I shouldn't get my hopes up but I was too excited to listen. Zach and I finished our conversation and I rested the phone receiver back in its cradle. I went to bed that night with butterflies dancing between my ribs.

I SAW HER FROM ACROSS THE ROOM. She was standing at the bar, a drink in her hand, a long, flowing black skirt and a black top gracing her form. Her eyes sparkled with speckled sunshine. She saw me and smiled and something bright and wonderful exploded inside me. A warmth of excitement flowed through my body and my feet moved me toward her. The sounds of the crowded club all blurred together, and my breathing and heartbeat were blaring in my ears. The walk from the middle of the floor to the bar seemed to take forever and be instantaneous all at once. Suddenly I was there next to her, giddy and beaming. We embraced.

  Some people give the kind of hugs that are deep and heartfelt. Betty Ann is one of those people. Feeling her arms around me in that instant made me feel like I was back where I belonged, and I wondered how or why I had drifted so far away. There were no thoughts in my head, only feelings of rightness and joy.

  Then we were saying our hellos and talking, and I can't remember the words, but I remember how they felt- fluid, bright, natural, and real. Aside from running into her at the mall almost two years earlier and then randomly seeing her once the previous summer, I hadn't been around Betty Ann since we'd broken up- but I wasn't thinking about that. I instantly forgot all the pain of the break-up as if it had never happened. I could zip the middle space up, and we could be right back where we were: in each other's arms where everything was good and beautiful and true.

  I was gazing into her eyes, getting more and more lost, when I felt a hand on my arm. My friend Trish tugged at my sleeve. She said there was someone who wanted to see me. I reluctantly let her pull me away. I didn't want to go, but I didn't want to be rude. I wanted to visit with my friends, but I didn't want to leave that spot, there, in the warm bubble at the bar.

Betty Ann smiled and giggled, saying it was okay and that she would see me later. I looked back once before Trish pulled me across the club. Our eyes met again. She was still smiling.

I don't remember playing the show. I think it went well. When the shows were bad, I usually remembered. I was high as fuck. I always smoked as much weed as possible before we played. It's such a cliché, but I wanted to turn off my mind as much as I could, so I could get lost in the music, so it could be a spiritual experience. When I was younger, I never took drugs to have a spiritual experience with music because playing music was the spiritual experience. But things had changed, and apparently, I wasn't so young anymore.

The show ended, and we probably packed up our equipment like we usually did and somehow Betty Ann and I left the 40 Watt together in my little red car.

The next thing I remember is standing on Zach's front porch, gazing into Betty Ann's bright, blue eyes.

I always stayed at Zach and Phillip's house whenever we played in Athens, and Betty Ann had come back with me to hang out after the show. I'd rung the bell, and we were waiting for someone to let us in. I remember that she looked so angelic under the naked single bulb that lit the porch, with the light dancing in her eyes and forming a bright wreath behind her head. I felt a swell of heat inside me. All the feelings I had for her that had been welling up inside me since the moment I first saw her at the bar earlier that night pushed to the edges of my skin and spilled out. My body moved to hers. I leaned down, our lips touched, and the butterflies in my stomach burst into flames. Time stopped. All sound disappeared. I couldn't feel my feet or the earth beneath me.

There was a noise on the other side of the door. The lock jangled, and the door creaked open. I pulled back and turned and there was Phillip, standing in the doorway. He smiled and greeted us. I felt nervous. I hoped that he hadn't seen us kissing. He knew I had a girlfriend.

Untitled (#12)

Cigarettes and weed and alcohol

And cigarettes and weed and alcohol

Tonight, we fall apart

Into pieces of each other

Go, go, and go

He'll be drinking for the 21st year in a row

I can't kiss her a hundred miles away

But here in another body I'm possessed to adore

I love what it is

I love what this is

Let's become

Dead to most

But alive to me

Winter, 1997

Twelvle (winter, 1997)

We were drinking beer from a bottle. Someone was rolling joints. I don't remember who all was there or how many of us there were, but I remember us all drinking and smoking and smiling and laughing. There was music on the stereo. There were happy faces all around. I remember sitting on the floor next to Betty Ann. Everyone had crowded into Phillip's bedroom. We seemed to hang out in there a lot.

The evening wore on. People left. Zach went to bed because he had to wake up early the next morning for school or work or something that gets people out of bed at an early hour.

And I kept drinking and smoking.

Betty Ann asked me to take her home. It was getting late, later than it already was- which was already late. I told her I would, but I didn't get up from the floor. She asked again. Then a few more minutes passed, and she asked again.

I kept stalling. Didn't she understand that I had more weed to smoke and more beer to pour down my throat? The joints and the bottles whispered, *just one more toke, just one more drink*. Each word was a promise to heal my soul, and I needed the healing. I could feel their words and promises deep in my heart. And they made me believe.

Each time she asked me if we could leave and I delayed, Betty Ann smiled and said something that illustrated what a patient person she is. Finally, on maybe the fourth or fifth time she asked, I relented. We got up off the floor, said our goodbyes, and stepped out into the freezing January night.

Betty Ann and I made out while we were waiting for the car to warm up. My hands roved over her clothes. I moved to touch her. *Not in the car*, she said. Then I wanted to be out of the car. My entire being was aching for her. I told her I was so wasted I couldn't drive, which was mostly true. But what was totally true, was that I wanted her, and at that moment, I wanted her so much that the short time it would take to get to her house felt like an unbearable eternity. So, probably convincing myself that I was telling the truth, at least a little, I proclaimed myself unfit for operating a motorized vehicle. She didn't disagree. Maybe she was feeling the same thing I was. I bet she knew things I never would. But, whatever the reason, she didn't say.

We got out of the car and went back to the house.

After pounding on the back door, shivering in the freezing cold, and waiting for what seemed like forever, Phillip, cloaked in sleep, came to the door and welcomed us back in. We snagged blankets and hurried to the front room where there was a soft, orange L-shaped fabric couch. A small TV sat on a cart that leaned against the far wall, next to a closet door I'd never seen opened.

There, on that icy January night, we had our own space, together in the lovely dark.

Untitled (#13)

I was there for five minutes, you were in for life. Who was there to tell us we were taking the wrong exit?

    An experiment of wills

    So much to say, one glance isn't enough

    Watch faith breathed out in a second

    Exhaled with the smoke that sets my soul at mid-tempo

    Looking up secrets that don't have expiration dates

    In a dream, I flew above you

    I never wanted to fly lonelier than I could walk

    No one else would come when the rainbow touched your lips

    I couldn't see its glory

    Content to stay on the ground and drown myself in small lakes

    I drank of your flesh and I was healed

Winter, 1997

13ThiRteEN

(Winter, 1997, continued)

The next day we awoke to rain falling from gray skies, splashing against the windows with an indifferent plop. Dull light filled the room. I looked at Betty Ann, lying on her side on the opposite section of the couch, her face alight with a sleepy smile.

Later, we were in my car, finally making our way to her house. The beauty and wonder of the night before were still ringing in my head but, the guilt was already setting in, so I knew I had to ruin it. I lit a cigarette and steeled my nerves. Then I told her I had a girlfriend. She mumbled a reply I can't remember. Her eyes dropped to her hands. I saw her fingers twisting in her lap.

Maybe I explained everything; that the girlfriend in question lived in Birmingham, but had lived near Atlanta when we started dating about two years ago, before she moved for a job, and about how we were still "together" although we hardly saw each other and when we did it was mostly a bummer and we didn't have fun or sex and the relationship was basically dead but neither person would admit it. Still, I had a girlfriend. No one had officially ended it. Maybe I told Betty Ann all of this. Maybe I tried to explain why I couldn't just let a new and free and wonderful relationship unfold between us and pull me into its brilliant center. Maybe I tried to tell her how I couldn't just let good things happen because I believed I didn't deserve them. Maybe I didn't say much of anything. I remember us exchanging a few more words or things that sounded like words but could have been just sounds trying to express feelings but that fell short because a sudden let down or shattering is like being pushed off a cliff while you were in the happiest moment of your life and you can't understand why you're suddenly upside down in midair, screaming in sorrow and terror, making just that sound because no words will do.

Then; silence, dreaded, horrible silence. I'd hit the ground. The cliff was far, far overhead, and nearly out of sight, and I was just lying there, straining for breath, waiting to die.

I don't remember the rest of the ride. I remember feeling cold and empty inside. I was sobering up and was feeling worse and worse by the minute. I knew I had to get loaded, and quick.

Thankfully, one of Betty Ann's roommates, or a roommate's friend, had some weed he shared with me that afternoon. It almost took the pain away. I didn't even know what the pain was or where it was from except that now I was a cheater and oh, that was probably it but no, this wasn't a new pain- this was the same old familiar, stabbing ache that was always there no matter what I did. But I think it was worse on that day. The inner self-hatred and scorn bubbled and swirled inside me and I couldn't get stoned enough.

It upset me, secretly, that the weed guy didn't offer me bowl after bowl after bowl, and oh, here are pills to go with the weed and lets each wash the pills down with a six-pack. That will make you feel better! Yes, that sounds like a wonderful idea! Thank you!

But that didn't happen. Mildly stoned and severely depressed, I decided to leave.

Betty Ann walked me to the door and kissed me goodbye. And it wasn't just a little, bye-bye peck, it was a kiss-like-it's-the-end-of-the-world-kiss. I don't know how long we stood there, wrapped in a sad and wonderful embrace as the rain splashed down around us. My heart told me to stay but I wouldn't let myself. How could I accept happiness, just like that? How could it possibly be that easy?

    And then I was back in my car, alone. She stood on the front porch and waved as I steered out to the road and drove away, her breath rising into the bitter winter air. I wonder what I was thinking at that exact moment. I wish I could remember.

Untitled (#14)

Exchanging eyes:

The first time   I traded old for new

In between – I got cataracts

The second time – I traded new cataract eyes for old, foggy lenses

Now – I can't see at all

Winter, 1997

4TEeeN (Late winter/early spring, 1997)

Sometime not-too-soon but not-too-long after I'd spent the night with Betty Ann, when the southern evenings were getting longer and warmer, I went to visit my girlfriend in Birmingham. We didn't have sex. It was an awkward and uncomfortable visit, and I left depressed and confused as usual. On the way home, I took fourteen ephedrine white crosses: little pills that my friends and I affectionately referred to as "gas station speed". Since I wasn't comfortable drinking and driving yet and I didn't have any weed or narcotics, it was the only way I could think of to catch a buzz and try to suppress my feelings at that moment instead of facing and working through them. However, the amount of trucker speed I consumed had the opposite effect and all my previously suppressed feelings assaulted me at once and there I was on I-20 east, blaring Stryper at full volume, screaming along to every word, crying my eyes out. I suddenly and impulsively decided I wanted to see my grandma, whose house was only a short detour away. I lit yet another smoke, took a slug of highly-caffeinated soda, and turned off on the next exit.

I was super emotional at grandmas. I think she sensed that something was up even though she never let on. I remember that later that evening when mom and I were talking about my visit with grandma, she had asked me why I went to visit her. I'd said something vague, probably shrugging and proclaiming that I didn't know. She'd replied by saying she guessed that sometimes you just want to go see your grandmother.

My heart was cracking and coming apart and I was looking for some comfort. Sitting there and talking with grandma for that little while had been comforting, but, as soon as I got out on those familiar country roads to head back to Mableton, Stryper was a blarin' and the tears and screams were a-flowin'. It was on that drive home I decided I had to come clean. I had to tell my girlfriend what I'd done. And while I was coming clean, I had to *get* clean.

Untitled (#15)

I never make a wish when I light my last cigarette

Your tomorrow is tonight, sunshine

    Why is whatever what I mean?

    Words don't come this late

    When it's too soon to fall in love

It's true if it is

I wish it was

    I laughed but I didn't make a sound

    I dreamed but I never walked in my sleep

    I poked out my eyes before I could see

5.6.1997

Fifff15-TeeN

(spring, 1997)

Maybe I'd had an epiphany. Maybe I was on my way to drawing a conclusion that was still years away. I felt like I had gone to a place I never wanted to go and that my active use of drugs, booze, and people, had taken me there. I'd become the guy I never meant or wanted to be.

I felt that I had done something that was alternately terrible, regrettable, and dishonest, but that was also beautiful and deep and amazing, thus making every thought and feeling that much more confounding. I knew I felt awful about violating my girlfriend's trust, but I also knew I was happy that I'd spent the night with Betty Ann. I keenly knew, deep in my heart, I was going overboard on my self-imposed guilt trip because that's what I believed I was supposed to do. It's what they taught me: when you do something you feel bad about or when you fuck up, you punish yourself until, one day, you somehow feel absolution and then you get on with your life.

And hopefully, you figure out why you did what you did. And, moreover, I wasn't even sure if Dani was still my girlfriend or not, even though I said she was, my heart kept questioning what was coming out of my mouth.

I thought I'd figured it out. Surely it was the booze and drugs that had turned me into a cheater. It wasn't because I was lonely and depressed and had a chemical imbalance in my brain, or that my heart burst with affection every time I saw Betty Ann or heard her voice or thought of her. No, those weren't my *real* feelings or issues; it couldn't possibly be that simple. And it wasn't that simple, because, when is anything simple or straightforward when you can't or won't let yourself think a simple or straightforward thought and you're not even sure what a simple of straightforward thought is anymore?

But at least I had a simple and straightforward plan of action to fix things and make my life right again and make myself not want to be dead. I had to make penance. I had to find forgiveness, and I needed new clothes and a haircut because apparently, my addictions had turned me into a real slob. Thus began my journey of repentance, and, my first actual attempt at Do-It-Yourself-By-Yourself sobriety.

Untitled (#16)

The glossy haze prevents fragments from forming into thoughts

I've wanted to die some (a lot) days

Last night was close enough

Death said, "Hi!"

And I shit my pants

Spring, 1997

SiXXX16tEEN

(spring, 1997)

Since this would be the first time I'd ever tried to stop drinking and smoking weed and taking pills and acid and shrooms and speed and whatever else was around, I did not understand what I was attempting. I thought, or assumed, that if you felt like stopping, you just did, and that was all there was to it. I'd seen friends and acquaintances and movie characters do it, so what was the big deal. It didn't seem to bother them. Still, I felt like I needed at least a little help because I knew getting and staying sober scared the shit out of me and that let me know something was wrong even though I didn't know what that something was. But I could mostly do it all on my own. I mean, I didn't need any meetings or rehab or anything like that, right?

After spending the afternoon at grandmas, I called Dani, my girlfriend, that evening. The speed was still zooming through my veins, taking my guilt to new heights, and I broke down weeping and told her everything. She sounded like she cried some too. I told her I felt like I had a real problem with drugs and alcohol. She was kind and gentle and didn't yell. She told me of a therapist she knew in my area that specialized in treating addicts since he himself had been in recovery for many years. Was I an addict? I mean, me, for real? I knew I liked to get fucked up all the time but what was wrong with that? My mind teetered back and forth between labels and phrases and notions and possibilities, not settling, only wandering in a murky fog of maybe.

I promised Dani that I would go to the therapist. I promised I would be faithful and never, ever cheat again. I made more promises I can't remember, trying with grand desperation to cling to the familiar. I pleaded with her to not break up with me. *I can fix this, I know I can.* She said she couldn't promise me anything. She said we'd have to wait and see.

After cradling the receiver of my classic black rotary dial phone, I fell on my knees next to my bed, tears raining down my face, begging for forgiveness, pleading for God to take away my pain, desperately wanting the lightning strike miracle I imagined would come and make everything better in one fell swoop, squeezing my eyes, contorting my face, snot dripping out of my nose, still high as fuck on cheap-ass gas station speed.

Untitled (#17)

I'll never profane this holiness again

        Turning from one

        To face the eternal

        Silence is a bland harmony that I accept

        For who or what I am

        With nothing to go forward to or back upon

        The sores on my feet can't be healed

        The broken life sentence can't save or return the part of my soul I gave to you

        How many times can I go about this giving and taking?

        Always losing

        Always learning

        Never changing

Spring, 1997

7vEnTeeen (Spring, 1997, again)

The next day or maybe the day after that, I was at my friend Ryan's house and Ryan, his brother Josh, and our friend Lee were all crowded into the bathroom with me. One of them had a pair of electric clippers and they were shaving my head. It was a symbolic act: off come the dreads and in comes a new life. As my dreads fell off into the sink with each swipe of the buzzing electric razor, I felt that at any moment I would feel free and new. And I waited, and waited, and waited some more. Time dragged the seconds and minutes by, kicking and screaming and protesting every step of the way. A blatant horror bubbled beneath my veneer of happiness and willingness to change.

I looked in the mirror. The dreads were gone but I was still there, and the feelings of worthlessness, shame, and despair were more visible than ever. I thought maybe there was no such thing as a magic haircut after all.

Lee laughed. "You look so stupid now!"

Josh ran his fingers over my freshly shaved head. "Yeah man, I can't believe you let us do that to you."

"It's symbolic," I said. "It's part of my repentance."

"You can repent all you want, but you'll never be happy. Things like this stick with you: they never go away," Lee said.

I felt like crying. "But, I'm really trying."

"It doesn't fucking matter," Josh said. "And you need to understand: it will never fucking matter."

"What?" I began. Josh cut me off when he grabbed the back of my neck and slammed my face into the sink. I squirmed under his grip, thrashing my arms back and forth. The severed dread locks wrapped around my throat and squeezed tight. I couldn't breathe. The locks snaked up to my lips and pushed into my mouth. Josh yanked me up and threw me into the tub. My back crashed against the tile as I fell, gagging on the lengths of hair creeping down my throat. I gagged and choked and pulled at my hair while Lee and Josh pointed at me and laughed. Tears poured out of the corners of my eyes. Just before I choked to death, Josh tapped me on the shoulder. "You okay, buddy?" He asked.

I sighed and inspected my shaved head in the mirror. I did look fucking stupid. "Yeah, I'm fine," I said, and I knew I didn't believe a fucking word of it, and Josh probably didn't either.

Now that I'd had my magic haircut, it was time to get back into church. I was all ready for God to fix me up, so I could finally get rid of my depression, stay off drugs and booze for good, and get my girlfriend back. My friend Ryan from Joe Christmas and some of our other friends had been going to this church over near the square, so I decided to go there too. After the bit of life I'd experienced, it felt weird being back at church; actually, it felt kind of wrong. But, I was looking to the familiar for a solution and church had helped me in the past. I believed in a spiritual solution and this seemed to be the most logical place to find it. I guess I couldn't really think of anything better. So, I went to that church twice a week, and when I wasn't at church, I was listening to my old Christian metal tapes on a constant loop, chain-smoking cigarettes, guzzling coffee, and praying to God to keep me off drugs and booze. It was a total white-knuckle fest, and it totally fucking sucked.

Then, with a strange suddenness, things got better. Betty Ann and I were talking and writing letters and, because she is an amazing, forgiving human being, it looked like we would salvage our friendship. Dani and I were talking and occasionally seeing each other, and I believed we might still have a future. I felt like some real healing was taking place inside me. I was feeling like I would get out of this one with no permanent damage or lasting effects. But deep down inside, a foreboding anxiety kept on growing. I walked outside and looked at the sky. It was bleak and dark and full of shoes; I stood still in place and waited for them to fall.

A few days later, the phone call came, and everything changed and would never, ever be the same again. I'd been watching TV with my parents. I don't remember what the show was; I think I was just staring at the screen while my mind was somewhere else. When the phone rang, my mom picked it up. She said it was for me. I told her I'd take it in my room and got up and left. It was Betty Ann. I was happy to hear from her. She asked me to sit down. I did. And I waited.

The line crackled.

She cleared her throat and said two words that are still ringing in my ears:

I'm Pregnant.

Untitled (#18)

I've wasted so much precious time

Wasted

Fucked up, going blind

You tried to hold my hand while I pulled away

To show up late where there was no party

Now my brain weighs heavy

Bleak pondering, the anti-Christ army

Walk on a wave

Lying with volcanoes

Is there really any other way?

Spring, 1997

8-TEEn (Spring, 1997, still)

After I got the news, I wrote a long, spiraling letter to Dani, in which I told her all the things I thought she wanted to hear, but which I also believed I meant, and maybe I did –I'm pretty sure I did, actually- and then at the end I dropped in a line about how Betty Ann was pregnant (hoping with all absurd and unrealistic hope that she somehow wouldn't notice or that maybe she would but because it was at the end of the letter she wouldn't mind it so much) but that I loved Dani so, so fucking much and hoped and believed we could work everything out if she would just give me another chance. I put the letter in the mail and waited.

Several days later the phone rang early one morning, pulling me from the fog of sleep, jarring me awake with fear. It was Dani. She wanted to know what my zip code was. What? I asked. She demanded the information. *What's your fucking zip code?* I rambled off the code. She said she was sending me a letter. Anger and hurt colored her words. She hung up. I rubbed my eyes and felt that familiar ache in my chest, below all the skin and bones, in the place no one can see. That day I didn't have any drugs or even any booze or cough syrup to take the pain away. I reminded myself that I wasn't relying on drugs anymore and that I'd just have to deal with it. I cursed myself for ever embracing such a horrible notion as sobriety.

Two days passed, and Dani's letter arrived. It said pretty much what I'd expected: *We were through.* It said so, right there on paper, in the handwriting of a strong and self-reliant woman. Even though I read it over several times, I'm not sure I believed it. Maybe that's why I found myself in my car, driving to Birmingham to see her so she could tell me in person. And that's when I learned that talking it out doesn't always fix things and that no matter how bad you want it to, sometimes words can't make it better.

Untitled (#19)

My heart is full of all the wrong things

Cigarette fed addiction

Trite and cliché

A faltering view from dim eyes

The movie screen has patches and holes

That block out the most romantic scenery

My eyes are closed

To the love around me

Just feel pity for someone

Who never had what he wished for

To dream and die escaping earth's pull

I forgot everything

Spring, 1997

9-tEEn (More of Spring, 1997)

The next night I was still in Birmingham and nothing had been resolved. We were at the apartment of a friend of Dani's. I can't remember who the girl was, but I do remember that I kept wondering what the fuck I was doing there, why I still insisted on hanging around, and why nobody was telling me to get the fuck out.

Dani's friend wanted to watch a movie called *Trainspotting*, which I'd heard of but hadn't seen yet. The three of us piled onto the girl's bed and she popped the movie into the VCR.

While the film played, thoughts tumbled and turned in my mind, about how I felt I'd ruined my life, and at twenty-one years old, I was ready to call it. The thoughts were big, hurtful boulders that made dents and cracks in my skull. I felt so fucking sick of everything. It was all bullshit. Life was a fucking waste of time. My list of failures and disappointments played on a loop in my head: Joe Christmas was breaking up and the last show was fast approaching. I would be somebody's dad and I had no college education because I'd dropped out, and I had no job, no way to provide for me or anyone else. Dani and I were done, and since that was over, there was no reason to stay sober because I'd gotten sober hoping we could stay together. I couldn't be any good to anybody, a worthless waste, Blah, blah, blah -on and on and on. It all circled around and around, spiraling in and out, over and over and over again. At the ultimate epic pity party, I was the guest of honor.

Dani's friend interrupted my endless train of woe-is-me by asking if we could stop the movie for a cigarette break. That sounded like a fantastic idea to us all, so we stepped out of the apartment and lit up. And there, standing on the stoop on that warm Alabama evening, puffing on a smoke, with scenes from the film playing in my mind, I knew I what I was going to do. I just had to find it first.

Untitled (#20)

I'm going swimming

Swim to the end of a beautiful nightmare

Wet and destroyed

Soaking in piss

Waiting for the fuck of a lifetime to set us free

Spring, 1997

Too-Ooh[20] (Even more Spring, 1997)

On a bright and sunny spring day, Betty Ann and I met up in Athens. It was the first time I'd seen her in person since she'd told me she was pregnant. Her hair was long and messy like she didn't give a fuck. She was wearing a tattered Dead Milkmen t-shirt. We'd walked along the sidewalk downtown and exchanged words I can't remember. I only remember feeling nervous and scared. Later, she told me she'd felt nothing but a bleak anger. There wasn't any resolution to the situation, only the acknowledgement. For me, there was no comfort or solution, only the same familiar emptiness inside.

As spring wore on, Betty Ann and I talked and wrote letters, trying to figure out what to do. Once on the phone, I made her cry. She hung up while I was making a pathetic attempt to apologize. Staring at the receiver, sadness and confusion overwhelmed me. And I didn't reach out for help. I kept it all inside. This was my pain, caused by a problem I'd created, and no one else needed to know about it. But it didn't have to be a problem, and it could've been a joy, and that summer could have been a beautiful time of wonder and learning and preparation, instead of me being scared shitless, hiding out, thinking my life was over because there was a new and unexpected adventure on the horizon.

Summer became fully realized, and I felt worse and worse until I gave up on everything. I became terrified to see Betty Ann again. I didn't call or write for I don't know how long. I saw her at the Marietta square one night and I hid in an alley. I couldn't face her. I was so filled with shame and horror I became immobile. All I wanted to do was to erase everything and start over. I wanted to not be an addict, and I wanted to have the courage to embrace my life. I wanted to know what the hell to do. I wished and wanted and hoped and prayed and didn't do shit to make anything any different, except lots and lots of drugs. My goal was to get as high as possible as often as possible. I was convinced that, in a state of inebriated contemplation, I could somehow find the answers I needed to fix everything and force life to make sense again.

∞InTerMiSsIoN∞

Fuck me Fuck me

Part III

I sit at the Pulpit of Dawn

Untitled (#21)

I wanna be a shut-in

I don't wanna see anyone

Sleep all day

And wake when the sun is hidden from the world

Smoke cigarettes until my black lungs shut off

Breathing becomes a dead task

Fuck myself until I bleed

And die in sobs that echo out of my dead, hollow heart

Summer, 1997

TwenTee2 1oNe

(summer, 1997)

I think the avoidance incident at The Square was the last time I saw Betty Ann before I met Hadley and started shooting dope. The summer was flying past me. Every day was a rush to get high in one way or another, to make the days disappear in an exciting blur. Hadley and I started sleeping together. Then we were together all the time, with our needles and our naked skin and grinning, droopy eyes. I was completely taken. Life felt magical, yet, I could still hear the small voice in the back of my mind, reminding me that none of it was real, that it was all an illusion that would implode under its own weight. But I wasn't listening. I couldn't listen even though part of me wanted to. The voice was loud at home, in my teenage room; too loud. I couldn't stand it, I needed to get out.

At some point that summer, I moved into the shack, the previously mentioned, infamous party house. I lived in the tiny two-room cottage with six other people. There were always drugs and booze and hardly anyone worked. I had a small succession of jobs while I was there. I ran food at a pizzeria on Peachtree until I got too lazy to drive down there -although the traffic afforded lots of great opportunities for drinking and slow-driving. Next, I worked at a donut shop in Austell. My one and only shift there lasted for about two hours. The owner fired me for being too slow. Maybe that was because of the Xanax bars I ate before I clocked in that day. They made it kind of hard to walk and pay attention and talk to people. I could see that my self-sabotaging skills were growing stronger every day.

    I somehow survived to see summer once again turn to fall, and I wasn't sure if I was happy about that or not.

Untitled (#22)

Life seemed easy

I thought I understood

Then on the day you touched me,

Everything new became ancient

The stories we told kept us warm inside

But now I'm dead

And only you can bring me back to life

The way you touch my mind

It makes me feel alive

Fall, 1997

TweNty2 (fall, 1997)

It was there at the shack, on my twenty-second birthday, sitting on the floor of the second bedroom, that I shot myself up for the very first time. And on that day, the dope gods looked down and said it was good. Hadley wasn't there that night. She'd broken off whatever we had after I'd tried to kiss one of our friends when I was drunk at a party.

One of Hadley's friends was at my birthday celebration, though, and she, being the elder user, was kind of overseeing the proceedings. She watched me tie off. I was using my dad's old brown leather belt. She watched me find and raise my preferred vein. She watched me stick the needle in and milk the blood. I breathed heavy through my nose and bit the belt. My eyes were wide. I felt the warming sensation flowing through me before I even pushed the plunger all the way in. And then the angels were singing again. I somehow got the needle out of my arm and the belt off. Was I sitting up or lying down?

Was everyone else okay? My friend Garret was there too. He and I often shot up together. I was happy he was there to celebrate my birthday with me. I was hoping he would be there until the end. I think I lit a cigarette. Then I was out on the front porch, puking my birthday dinner of burgers and fries up over the railing.

        On the inevitable day that all of us left the shack the same nice girl who had watched over me on my birthday and made sure I didn't die that night, helped me pack up the old Joe Christmas tour van and move all my belongings back to, once again, my old room in my parents' house. After everything was inside my room, we sat down on the end of my bed and breathed in the silence. I asked what we were supposed to do next. I don't remember if I was talking to her or to myself.

        I think she left, and I tried to find drugs of some sort. I don't think I ever saw her again after that day and I still can't remember her name or if I ever really knew it. But I remember *her*. And, if I ever see her again during my life and if she remembers who I am, I want to thank her for being kind and making sure I didn't accidentally overdose on my birthday.

Untitled (#23)

I have to get loaded to feel my heartbeat

    Check my pulse with a **need**le

Get back in

It wasn't your birthday

    There was a dream I woke up trying to remember

    I was listening, but all your words were in Spanish

    I couldn't read your moving lips

    Fixed eyes

    Hollow expression

    I love you more

    Than these people or things

    That time melts and fucks away

    I wish I still knew you

Fall, 1997

TWenTy-3 (winter, 1997)

Christmas had come around again. Parker was just over two months old and my heroin use was taking off - I was almost ready to go full-time. Even though I was working around forty hours a week in a kitchen, deep-frying giant onions and washing dishes, I was broke because all my money was going straight into a needle. By the time Christmas Eve arrived, the only person I'd bought a gift for was Joy, my dealer. I'd gotten her some kind of cutesy coffee mug hoping if I gave her a present, she'd totally hook me up when I went to her house to score on Christmas night. I had already made plans with Joy and her nephew, who everyone called Nephew, two days before the twenty-fifth so they knew to expect me.

I told my sister Amy and her boyfriend, Leon, that I had no presents for anyone but Joy, or any money to buy any more presents, and I didn't tell them about my secret dope money stash. They understood my plight and took me shopping at the local big box super-mart on Christmas Eve. Luckily, since the mega-store had pretty much everything, I could get one gift for everyone. I promised Amy and Leon that I would pay them back but I'm sure I never did, and I don't know if they remembered to ask me about it. I'm sure we got wasted on something that night.

On Christmas morning I was alone in my room cutting my left arm with a pair of dull scissors. That was new, but it felt good and right. I was on my third cut when my mom called for me, saying that Betty Ann and Parker had just arrived. I sighed and tried to pull my soul up from the black pit it was in. I looked at the cuts. They were shallow and barely even bleeding.

"You fucking pussy," the cuts said to me, "you can't even cut right."

While the wounds on my arm laughed at me, I pulled my shirt sleeve down and cursed my life. I told myself that I needed to get through the day, then I could go to see Joy and she'd make it all better. I never thought about what would happen the day after that, or, if I lived, the day after that one. I went into my closet and looked at my needle, imagining it was already full and overflowing. Then I put it back in its hiding spot and dragged myself out of my room to face the day.

I don't remember what happened that day except that it was awful and I hated it and I hated Christmas. Growing up, though, I had always loved Christmas. There was something magical about the cold and the lights and the stillness. Now the only magic was in a spoon.

After Betty Ann and Parker spent time with my family, we left and went to the family gathering at Betty Ann's grandma's house. My only memory from that gathering is a single image of walking down the stairs, and of the house being warm and cozy and comfortable. I couldn't wait for the day to end so I could get to Echo Street. I was counting every single minute. When it was over, Betty Ann drove me back to my parents' house. On the way, I told her I'd been doing heroin for a few months. I told her it was important that I'd like to share with her and that I'd like for her to ride down to Joy's with me. She wasn't into it. When got to my parents' house, I lied to my mom and dad about needing to go to the store or something and I left. When I got back home, Betty Ann and Parker were gone. My dad was in bed and my mom was in the back room watching a Hallmark Christmas movie. I asked where Betty Ann was. Mom told me she went home. Utterly and completely relieved and not really surprised, I said goodnight to my mom and went to my room to shoot up.

It turned out that Joy had totally hooked me up that Christmas. For $80 she had sold me a literal rock of dope. It looked like a white marble without the rounded edges. Nephew had brought it out in his bare hand and I'd gotten it home safe by stashing it in a cassette case. That night, alone in my room with Enya playing on my tape deck, I carefully rested the little rock on a small plate, shaved a piece off, and put the chunk in my spoon. It broke down easy and clear and when it hit my bloodstream Christmas became, once again, the most wonderful time of the year. I was so high I called my cousin in California and lamented to him about how shitty my life was. This was something I did a lot, and he always stayed on the phone and listened. I wonder if I ever thanked him for doing that.

The next day, when for some stupid reason I told them about how Joy had good Christmas dope, Amy and Leon got upset with me for not sharing with them. I didn't care. Although they'd totally bailed me out when I had no money, except my secret dope money, and no presents, I felt no need to share with them. That was my Christmas dope: why didn't they have their own?

On New Year's Eve, I could hear the party at Amy and Leon's all the way over in the living room of the big house. It sounded like they were having a real fucking blast. I was alone with no heroin or coke or speed or booze or pills or anything, trying to get stoned off the resin in my weed pipe. I had no money. I was skipping work. I'd isolated myself. I avoided phone calls and sat in the dark, thinking about how I deserved to be dead, wishing I were.

The next morning I saw Garret stumbling out of the guest house, shielding his eyes from the sun. I pulled on my cigarette and said hello. He asked me why I hadn't been over at Amy's the night before. I shrugged and mumbled an excuse I can't recall. Then I felt nothing but pure regret as he told me how awesome it was, and that they'd been mainlining Morphine and smoking the best weed he could remember. When I went to work at the restaurant the following day, I was nervous they would fire me as soon as I walked in because I'd called out on New Year's Eve. I fucking hated that job, but I needed it for the dope fundage. But I didn't get fired. One of my work friends told me it had been a great night, that everyone was in a festive mood, that the entire shift had gone smoothly, and that they'd even had a champagne toast at midnight. Then I realized that I could've gone to work, made money, had fun, and still gotten home in time to party with Amy, Leon, Garret, and the rest of my friends. I fumed. After work, I went home and sat in the dark just like I'd done on New Year's Eve. Life sucked, and I felt like there was nothing I could do about it. Well, there was one thing…

Untitled (#24)

High-heel eye fuck

Porn star

Cum shot

Self-mutilation grin

A gorgeous treat

Let the scissors split your skin

Give up and fuck yourself up your own ass

Cut off your own dick

Put it in your own mouth

Let your eyes water with blood

Cleanse myself sick

Mutilation

Flesh excavation

Person fuck

Shit love

Christmas, 1997

2TwenTee4 (Early winter, 1998)

They were all there, waiting for me in the back room. By the time I realized I'd been ambushed, it was too late.

I can't even remember why I walked back there. Maybe I was going to tell my parents I was going out because that's the polite thing to do instead of just leaving? Betty Ann and Parker were visiting, and I'd told her one of the usual lies about needing to go get cigarettes or something. I was all ready to go score some dope. I had money in my pocket and my keys in my hand.

My first thought when I saw the assembled group was: *why is my parents' church pastor here?* Then I noticed that Betty Ann's eyes were full of tears. I felt my feet start to shuffle backward. I think my dad asked me to come in and sit down. I started to get what was going on. I couldn't believe they were doing this! The one time I'd told my dad that I had a drug problem and that I needed help, he had dismissed me and said that it was all just in my head. He said that I just liked drugs a lot, but that surely, I couldn't possibly have a problem, or be an addict. But, there they were. I guess he'd changed his mind.

My dad was the first to speak. He told me they wanted to help me, and that they wanted me to go to a rehab facility. I considered running out screaming, but by this time Betty Ann was crying, and it broke my heart into a billion pieces to see her there sobbing on the couch with little tiny Parker in her arms. My son and his mom needed me and all I could think about was scoring dope and trying to forget about everyone and everything. All I was doing was causing them pain. With this in mind, after the pastor rattled off some pastorly shit, I agreed to go. I hugged Betty Ann and Parker and then I got in the car with my dad and he drove me across town and checked me in.

We arrived after dark. The rehab center was quiet. I don't remember how long my dad stayed there with me. A nurse or some kind of medical professional took my vitals. They assigned me a room. There was a creepy young guy who told me he was in for a pill addiction. He banged his head against the wall. I was informed that he would be my roommate. The next day, he ran out the door like he was a key player in a prison break. An employee shook her head in exasperation, saying he didn't have to run like that, he could've just signed himself out.

My first night at the facility, I wandered into something that looked like a break room. There was a phone. A cute girl was using it. She was crying. Several minutes later, while I imagined having sex with her, falling in love, and having a tortured romance, she explained she'd been shooting dope for five years straight. She'd been on the phone with her boyfriend. No, he wasn't coming to get her. She was visibly scared. She cried some more, and I felt bad for her, but I couldn't stop imagining what her naked breasts would taste like in my mouth.

I went to the group therapy sessions. I smoked outside in the designated smoking area. I analyzed and critiqued the people around me and told myself that I was not like them; that I was different. *They're sick, like, seriously sick,* I thought. *There's nothing wrong with me. I shouldn't be here.*

Three days later, convinced I was fine and well, I checked myself out and left the rehab center. When I hopped into the back seat of my sister's beat-to-shit blue car, Garret was in the front passenger seat. He smiled and said hello. I smiled back. We had a joint lit before we were out of the parking lot.

Untitled (#25)

I can't force-feed

Words onto this open-mouth page

Hand jerk

Masturbate my vocabulary

I can't make them cum

Force a feeling

Of being alive

Pushing out health and vitality

Systems shut-down

I'm struggling to feel

To sort through blank spaces

Her life is under reconstruction

I wish she'd build something with me

A minimalist's effort

Work of art

Frame house with no inhabitants

> I want to live there

I hate my house

> I hate the housekeeper
>
> I want a new life
>
> But is this what you'd expect me to say?

Ridgeview Institute
Jan. 4, 1998

TweNtee5

(Winter/spring, 1998)

After my brief and illuminating stay at the rehab facility, I embraced denial as a logical and sensible way to cope. Before going in, I had admitted that I had a problem and had even made a feeble attempt at asking for help. But then, three days later, I knew better: I didn't have any problems. I enjoyed drugs, and what the fuck was wrong with that?

The rest of the winter and the whole of the spring are a blurry stop-start of using every substance available, being seized by sudden and intense regret, trying to quit on my own, being unsuccessful, then repeating the whole cycle over again, disproving everything I'd thought when I left rehab. I saw Betty Ann and Parker now and then when I became overwhelmed by a flood of sentimentality or maybe it was my true nature coming through and, for a moment, overriding the addict mind protocol.

I remember going to see them one night when I was high on LSD and heroin. I stared at Parker, his eyes bright, full of curiosity and joy, and I couldn't believe how beautiful and perfect and happy he looked. I guess I was detached, though. I couldn't make the connection that he was my son and I should look after him because that's what you do. I remember those moments, when I wanted to be an active dad, and it seemed possible, like I was actually capable. But I never believed that for long. I would hear the hateful chorus screaming in my mind, telling me I couldn't take care of anyone, not even myself, crushing all belief into dust.

It amazed me that Betty Ann, and I had created him. Out of that passionate night came this wonderful little person. It truly blew me away. I sat there and stared and felt all warm and fuzzy inside.

Then it was time to go. Betty Ann and Garret and I were going to see Low play at The Point that night. I think Betty Ann drove us there. I puked in the parking lot before we went into the club. I don't remember the show at all, although I think I was conscious for it, which is better than the first time I went to see Low and came to on the floor with the house lights on and people stepping over me as they made their way to the exit because the band had played, it was over, and

I'd missed the entire thing. That evening was actually a great metaphor for my life: Parker was growing up and it was all flying by while I was loaded, passed out on the floor.

Untitled (#26)

Life was a series of highs

> Movement with no destination in mind

> Estranged coffin sleepers

> Walkers with fucks for heads

> I saw the shit and said that it was good

> I didn't know that I had been rubbing it in my eyes.

> Slippery promises

> Like a wet cunt

> Do you want to get fucked or not?

> Slippery promises

> Like a wet cunt you can't seem to get inside

> Because it's too dark to see

> I wish I'd never touched you fucking girls

Spring, 1998

Twenty-six666

(summer, 1998)

Somehow, I had once again survived winter and spring and was shambling into summer. All my friends told me the zombie look suited me. They especially liked the hollow eyes. Those had been very eventful months full of something that resembled living. I'd even recorded an ambient noise record with my good friend Garret and we'd played a live show at the Somber Reptile. I suppose that I was trying to hold on to the things that made me happy - making music, writing, making art, playing shows- but the drugs kept taking up more and more space and time, crowding everything else out, even though I was attempting to become more skilled with multi-tasking, i.e.; combining drug use with music making, and why not, it had usually worked in the past, right? But those were different drugs, and I was a different person. I guess heroin makes some people a better guitar player, but I wasn't one of those people. And eventually I didn't even have an amp to play my guitar through; I'd sold it to a friend for $30 so I could score a bag of dope; one fucking bag for the amp I had used to record North to the Future, the second and final Joe Christmas album. A single bag of dope. One dose. God-fucking-dammit.

I'd gone to buy heroin on Easter and seen my dealer in her Sunday best. I'd had week-long road trips in the name of sobriety that ended back at my dealer's house, giving the appearance that all roads led to Echo Street.

I'd been blessed and prayed over by self-aggrandizing saints and recovering alcoholics, I'd been talked with and to and at, and through it all nothing had convinced me to put down the bottle or the pill or the joint or, especially, the needle and the spoon.

And now it was June 1998, and my friend Stubs had invited me to go to Cornerstone, the much-beloved and fabled Christian music festival of my innocent youth, held in the wild fields of a small southern Illinois farming town every Fourth of July weekend. Because I'd often called him and droned into the phone while wasted out of my mind, Stubs knew I was junked out and so he offered to pay for everything if I would drive us up there. I hoped in my heart that going to Cornerstone would fix me. I'd go to the festival and God would move and I'd get cleansed and renewed, and head home with a healed heart. It was just the miracle I needed.

Seeing an opportunity to use a fellow human being under the guise of friendship, I mean, seeing an opportunity to spend time with a friend and get clean, I agreed to go.

Stubs and I were in the car, at the beginning of a twelve or fifteen hour drive, or however long it took to get there, and I got worried because I had less than a quarter ounce of weed and, even though I'd only ever experienced mild dope sickness up to that point, what if it would be worse this time? I mean, I'd been shooting up more and more. What if I really, seriously hurt? Would the black hole in the center of my chest suck me in and wring me inside out? I sat there in the driver's seat and wished I could be happy and excited about the trip, about going to what used to be my favorite place in the world, but I just felt miserable.

We stopped and spent the night at Zach's house in Athens. Stubs wanted to talk about one of Zach's old bands. Zach got annoyed. He wanted to know why I was hanging out with this guy Stubs, why I brought him to Athens, and why the fuck was I going to Cornerstone? After growing out of Christian music and Christianity it seemed absurd to Zach that I would go back to that festival again. That was somewhere we went when we were kids. Maybe I still wanted to be a kid. I was reaching, desperately hoping for something to make me not want to die, to find a clue or a meaning or a way to save my life and make me happy again. I wanted an answer. But I couldn't explain this to Zach, so I shrugged and mumbled something or another that didn't really make any difference and it still annoyed him but he let us stay the night. The next morning, we were back on the road with the sun in our eyes and black soot in my heart.

That night we drove into a storm somewhere in Tennessee. We were blasting the *X-Files* movie soundtrack at top volume while lightning slashed across the sky and thunder roared above us. We rolled down the windows. Gusts of wind swooped down and rocked my small red car. My eyes were wide. Gooseflesh covered my body. Despite the ever-present sinkhole in my spirit, I felt the magic of the storm and the mystery of the night. And then we needed food and coffee. We stopped at a diner. The storm had knocked out their power, but they still had lukewarm coffee and food from the gas grill. I don't remember what we ate but I remember that it was good. An hour later Stubs and I were back out on the road and, by dawn, as the sun reclaimed the sky from the night, we zoomed down the country roads of Bushnell, Illinois, heading for the festival grounds. By mid-morning, we had our tent stakes in the dirt and it was time to check out some Christian rock. Hell fucking yeah.

I spent the entire festival hoping someone would notice me and say *hey, aren't you the guitarist from that one band?* And trying not to feel like killing myself while having the occasional moment of fun. I'd smoked up my weed stash by the end of the first day. I scraped my pipe and smoked resin for the rest of the trip. I ended up in a bar with twenty-five cent drafts of the shittiest beer ever. I went to visit friends who lived nearby in Peoria. Seeing their happy family made me want to slash my wrists and bleed out in their cul-de-sac. Every single thing I did, every moment of that trip, I felt like I was outside looking in. I wanted desperately to feel included but I felt like I had a secret that created a force field around me and kept everyone away. I looked at my friends with their happy lives and I felt like I was the other. They hadn't gotten anyone pregnant. They didn't have a kid. They weren't running from their lives; they were present and they were glad. Well, fuck them. Months later, reflecting on that weekend, I imagined that I'd gone to the fest with a massive, trafficking-size supply of dope and needles and cigarettes, enough to keep me as comfy and cozy as I wanted to be. My belly would glow with warmth at the thought and I'd fantasize about how wonderful my trip to Cornerstone would have been if I could've been high the whole time. Oh, how perfect that would have been.

On the last night at the fest, I made out with an old friend who might have one day become a girlfriend. We watched fireworks together. She said she liked the way I touched her. Her lips were golden honey, but I only wanted her to take my pain away. After we kissed and let our hands roam over each other, we laid silent and still and listened to the sounds of the night and the festival that surrounded us. The pain and guilt and shame rushed back, bearing down, pushing and contorting my soul. And in that horrible moment, I wanted heroin more than anything in the world because I had a special pain that only a special something could wipe away. I stopped wanting freedom and only longed for comfort.

My spirit ached and cracked and broke. My friend and I said goodbye in the sunshine of the new morning. I hated myself. Weeks later, we talked on the phone. She cried when I told her about the drugs. I wanted to cry with her, but no tears came. I was numb.

On the way back home from the last Cornerstone I would ever attend, Stubs and I stopped and stayed with Zachary again. This time, I found the Xanax that Zach had hidden in his sock drawer. Four Xanax bars and a joint later and Stubs and I were on our way to his house on the south side. Maybe there was traffic in Atlanta that afternoon, but I didn't mind. Although they never got me high the way I wanted them to, Xanax pushed the special pain into another room of my soul where I couldn't see it as much. I didn't feel good, but I didn't feel totally suicidal. I didn't really feel much of anything at all. After Stubs was safely dropped off at his house, I got back in my car, buckled up, and wondered what the fastest route to Echo Street would be.

There were four twenties in my front left pocket. Before we'd even left for Cornerstone, I knew I had to come home with these eighty dollars. I'd made a deal with myself that, no matter what, Stubs could never know I had that money -sacred money I could only spend on one thing. I knew the entire trip I wasn't trying to get off the shit even though that's what I'd told myself and everyone else; I was just forcing myself to take a break, a miserable, awful, pointless break. And now the break was over, the wait was through, and half an hour later I was pulling into my dealer's driveway.

Untitled (#27)

Bury your loved ones in a h**O**le

In your mouth, there's a small plot for everyone

Tend the garden but leave the weeds

Give up before you start

Bury every memory

Let the glowing sun weep for lost dreams

Of how you used to be a poet

Or something or someone else

-Who used to make friends laugh-

And make friends last

Summer, 1998

2wentee7 (Mid-summer, 1998)

I don't remember who came out to the car that night. Maybe it was Joy- the lady of the house, Pookie- Joy's live-in boyfriend, or Nephew- Joy's nephew. I always preferred to deal with Joy; I liked her best. In fact, I had a genuine affection for her as a person. Even though we had a dealer/customer relationship, I always thought of her as a friend, or maybe a kindly, part-time grandmother of sorts. She was always reliable too. When I first learned about how her business operated, I was skeptical that it would be in any way dependable, which made me nervous because I wanted to get my shit when I wanted to get it. It was simple though; you'd just pull up to the house –you could go at pretty much any time of night- and wait. They must have been on the look-out, though, because when you swung up into the short, hilly driveway, the car's headlights would wash over the small house, and, usually almost immediately, one of the three of them would shuffle out onto the porch, lean over the vine-covered railing, and ask you what you needed. It was a simple and effective set-up: curbside service, sometimes even with a smile.

It was a perfectly muggy July evening when I pulled up in Joy's driveway. Thick, wet summer air wafted into the car when I rolled down the window. I asked for four bags. They said they'd be right back. Sometimes they took a while to bring you the dope because they'd have to walk down the street to another house to get it. Sometimes it only took two minutes because they had it in their house, all bagged up and ready to go. But, no matter what, long or short, just like the song says, you always had to wait.

In my experience, any substantial amount of Xanax in the system plays funny tricks with time. I felt like I had only been there for a few seconds, leaning back in my seat, listening to the traffic swooshing down Bankhead a block away and the crickets singing in the bushes nearby, not a thought in my head, when whoever I'd spoken to suddenly materialized at my door. They leaned down. I held out my hand. They dropped four small blue plastic bags into my palm. Once the dope was in my hand, I felt the familiar excitement bolt through me. *Oh shit, I got it!* I handed over my eighty bucks, thanked my dealer, and shoved the little bags of powdered wonder deep down into my sock and under my foot. I always put it in my right sock. That seemed to be the safest place. I pulled out of the driveway and drove back out into the night. I couldn't wait to get home where I could be alone, just me and my drugs and some music and soft light and no thoughts or worries or cares in the world. And everything would be all right once again, at least for a little while.

I don't remember much about the rest of the night. I made it back home without crashing or getting arrested. I must have unpacked the car because I usually never left anything in the car after a trip. I remember that the light in the kitchen was low. My sister was there. She said mom and dad had already gone to bed. It must have been later than I thought. She asked me to hang out and have a beer with her in the back room. I told her that'd be great; I just needed to take a shower first. She said she'd be waiting for me and told me she was glad I was home. I lied and said I was too. I wasn't glad to be anywhere, but I had something in my sock that was about to make it not matter where I was.

I went to the bathroom I used to share with my sister and locked both doors. I retrieved my freshest needle and my favorite spoon from their hiding spot in the bottom drawer on my side of the bathroom counter. I slid my favorite Dead Can Dance tape into the radio and pressed play. The soothing music filled the small room. I sat cross-legged in front of the toilet and rested my tools on the mustard yellow lid.

Even though I hadn't been using that long, I'd already perfected my own personal ritual. I had the lighting set soft and low; I had the dreamy music on at a minimal yet listenable volume. I had my trusty scissors that my dad had bought me to use with my remote-control car when I was ten years old. They made the scissors to cut and shape the plastic body and parts of the race car. I had built and owned two kits and I'd thought one day when I was older, I'd race RC cars professionally, because people do that, you know, and it would have been a super fun way to make a living. I also had the tattered old brown leather belt that my dad had given me. Parts of it were being held together with duct tape. Every time I tied off with it I remembered how I told myself that I would not use it, not *this* belt, to tie off with, because my dad had given it to me, and I could still remember seeing him wearing it when we'd be out working in the garden on Saturday afternoon.

I had my special spoon I'd pilfered from the kitchen set (my mom had never missed it) and my trusty brown plastic cup -the one from the old plastic lunch tray set that the whole family used to eat with on Saturday afternoons while we all watched PBS together when I was a little kid- and I had my B&D 1 CC insulin syringe with the bright orange cap, the simple implementation that would deliver the glory into my veins and bring me closer to God and universal truth and understanding, or maybe just get me fucked out of my ever-living mind.

My heart raced, my palms sweated, and my entire body tingled with anticipation as I began my self-surgery ritual.

First, I had to use my scissors to open the bag because they always burned the top to seal it shut. The sharp blade cut the burned plastic, and I pulled the seal apart to reveal the love inside. I dumped the first bag into the spoon and then repeated the process with a second. Once I'd emptied the two bags of powdered joy into the spoon, I filled my syringe up to the 10 mark. I squirted water into each bag to rinse out any remaining residue and then dumped the water into the spoon. A murky white formed in the spoon's belly. When the bags were clean, it was time to mix. The plunger made a "pop!" when I pulled it free from the needle. Holding the spoon steady by the handle, I stirred the dope and water mixture until the white powder dissolved. I grinned at the clear liquid in the spoon. I grabbed my scissors and sliced off the tip of the filter from one of my cigarettes, ripped off the light brown paper, and balled the filter up between my fingers. With a hand that shook with expectation, I dropped the tiny ball of the filter into the sacred nectar. I always loved this part, watching the filter hit the solution and darken and expand as it sucked up the magical potion. Quivering with anticipation, I pressed the tip of the needle into the filter and drew the elixir up into my rig, careful to extract every drop from the spoon, watching the filter turn a bone-white as it dried out. Some of my friends would put the filter in their mouth and suck on it like a candy but I never did, at least not that I can remember.

While Brendan Perry crooned softly in the background, I wrapped my father's old brown leather belt over my skin, looping and tightening it above the crook of my right arm. My entire body buzzed with excitement. It was the moment I'd waited for.

I put the free end of the belt between my teeth. I bit down and pulled. I squeezed my fist.

My knuckles whitened, and my veins bulged. I saw it, my favorite vein, raised in the crook of my arm. My hand, now steady, lowered, holding the needle, my thumb on the plunger as a finger on the proverbial trigger, happiness, and the warm gun, sunshine and the boy, ready to explode my senses and pull me under into its glowing embrace.

Perry hit a high note and held it. I pushed the needle in and pulled the plunger back. Blood rushed into the chamber. I pulled the plunger back further. More blood flooded in. Then I pushed, slowly and deliberately, and the wonderful, beautiful warmth, the soothing light of all that is good, poured over me like the Light of the Lord, a pure revelation, a welcoming, comforting rebirth. I felt it coming up from the center of my soul, in my belly, in my center, and then it was in my brain and all around me and I was still moving the plunger toward its final destination at the needle's tip, still pushing gently, still urging, and still growing. Brendan Perry's voice faded into the distance. I saw the yellow and gold 1970s wallpaper that my parents still hadn't replaced even though they said it was ugly, swirling and bending sideways. I saw the dim light from the bathroom's exhaust fan shining down on me. I saw the toilet in front of me. Then I saw nothing at all: Captured in the depths, floating weightless in the in-between, wading through nothing, not seeing, feeling, hearing, or knowing. I had returned to the womb. Three days later, I came to in a hospital bed.

Untitled (#28)

Fucked up

  In conflict with grandfather clocks

  Spinning arms, gears slip and stall

Spill into a cotton

Pull up the life

  A clear view

  Pull up to color the clear

Hold my breath and push in the serenity

Fold over to cover and cleanse

  I can hear for miles

  A whispered tranquility

Beauty in a motion

  A dim-eyed waking dream,

  Living in a time-lapse drone

Summer, 1998

Tw2eEnty-8 (Miserable Mid-summer, 1998)

My throat felt like I had gorged myself on a buffet of glass and rusted razors. A man in the corner was whispering. Dark, murky shapes flickered in the hazy air. Rough fabric draped over me like a loose curse. A sheet of yellow-stained light slid under the closed door. The man's quiet voice came as a foreign language. Then I recognized the language as English. I had no idea what he was saying. My eyes scanned my dark surroundings. I didn't know where I was, or why I was there, or how I got there. Maybe the pain in my throat was a clue. I should have been in my house, in my room, not wherever this was. Maybe I dreamed that I'd woken up, and I really was at home in my room, in my bed. The man lit a cigarette, and the cherry burned orange under his nose as he inhaled, casting a weak glow over his face. He exhaled and mumbled some more lost words. The reek of smoke filled the small room. I rolled over and everything went black again.

Sifting through this section of my memories is like having a pile of photograph fragments that could form a picture but there just aren't enough parts to make a complete whole. Everything I remember about that room is dim and hazy. My only clear memories seem to come days later, after I'd fully come to and been told that I had overdosed and was in the hospital. I don't remember what they called the unit I was in, but it seemed to be a separate building out behind the main hospital. I was there with a small group of people. Maybe they had overdosed too?

The staff was jaded but kind. Maybe they meant it when they told me I was lucky to be alive and that I needed to be thankful.

I learned that my throat was all shot out because they had pumped my stomach in the ER, which apparently required shoving a tube down my throat, emphasis on the shoving. I also learned that my mom had been there the whole time, watching her only son being pulled back from the Great Goodnight, being forced to puke up all the bad stuff, wailing and crying and cursing, out of my mind. Thinking of that, of her watching me, that I caused her to be in that position, fills me with a dreadful awe and a dark numbness I can't articulate. I imagine her standing with my father, under the harsh hospital fluorescents, her hand over her mouth, her eyes watering behind her glasses as she watches the scene unfold, hating to look but not being able to turn away. I wonder what she was thinking during those moments, or if she was thinking anything at all. And how did my parents feel when, after the lifesavers stabilized me and wheeled me away to a room, it was time for them to go home because there was nothing more they could do there? Did they talk on the way back to the house? When they got home, did they take a nap or watch TV? Were they glad I was still alive? Was I?

My next memory is of being outside in the sun, having a smoke and feeling fine. Then I was playing basketball on the small court out behind the facility and thinking to myself once again that I didn't have a drug problem at all, I'd just had an accident, and that I couldn't wait to get high again. I remembered that I still had two bags of dope waiting for me at home. I'd have to be more careful, though; didn't want to wind up in this shithole again. My body felt great, I was okay, and everything was all right. I was sure I'd be going home soon and that my life would be back to normal. I wondered how Joy was doing. I was sure I'd see her again soon.

And then a group of murmuring doctors and EMTs appeared and surrounded me. I sensed that I might not be going home so soon after all.

The ride to the new facility wasn't so bad. I guess it was kind of interesting. I was being transferred, almost like a prisoner. I suppose I was a special case because I'd almost killed myself and all that fun stuff. I was in the back of an ambulance. Two EMTs sat on the bench across from me. I tried to make small talk, but it didn't work. I guess they weren't much for conversation. About a half hour later we arrived at the Crisis Stabilization Unit. After being checked in and assigned a room, I walked over to the window. My new roommate was enthusiastically belting out a country pop song. He had a lisp that might have made his singing hilarious under different circumstances.

I peered through the rusted metal mesh that covered the windows to keep the patients from leaping out, hoping for an escape, preferably death, or even mild injury, or any fucking thing that would take them somewhere else. I watched a nurse crossing the parking lot. It looked like she was heading for her car. It was late in the afternoon and she was probably leaving work for the day. I watched her and thought about how I'd give anything to have that kind of freedom, just to go to work and drive home and do normal things and not need drugs or booze to help me do those normal things. I ran my fingers over the metal that separated me from the outside world and I knew then what it was like to feel truly, totally alone.

Untitled (#29)

Call the paramedics!

So afraid, I can't write

Become **still**

Make your **dead poet confession**

    (Keep writing and writing in circles)

    (Wondering why things have to change)

Why do we have to be like this?

What unseen, eternal force is twisting our arm?

Into compliance

We are forced

With no one bothering to ask us

What it was

That we actually wanted

Summer, 1998

TwenTy-9 (Mid-summer nightmare, 1998)

I don't remember exactly where the stabilization unit was, and I don't recall if I ever took the time to find out. I don't remember how long I was there. Maybe it was one week, maybe it was two. How do the authorities determine how much time is needed to "stabilize" an individual who has survived a drug overdose, or maybe another someone who tried on suicide, but it didn't fit like they'd hoped it would and now they're on the top floor of some fucking hospital, eating shitty food, having shitty conversation, and feeling generally shitty? Again, I kept thinking I wasn't like those people and that I didn't need to be there. I'd just had an accident, that was all. Why was everyone taking it so seriously?

There were group meetings. In one session, an older man

became so enraged that he stormed out of the room and checked himself out of the hospital altogether, declaring that there was no hope for him and that he had a full bottle of vodka in his trunk he needed to see right away. It had secrets to tell him. It would make everything okay again.

There was a young woman on the floor I despised. She told the group she was there to detox off pain pills because she'd accidentally gotten a little too familiar with Mr. Vicodin after her surgery. As she shared one day in the group, my imagination carried me away.

"Vic was so good to me," the attractive young woman cooed, sliding one hand down her shorts while running her other hand over her breasts. "He knew how to touch me in all the right places."

I saw it in my mind: Vic -the six foot something, chiseled pill. He was with her in the shower, rubbing against her. She moaned as the water splashed over her and trailed down between her breasts and her belly to her mystical triangle. Vic's massive hardness bulged and throbbed against her. He turned her around and slid his girth up and down between the cheeks of her ass. She couldn't wait to take him in even though she'd just had him not two hours earlier. She wanted him inside her all the time. It was what she needed: Vic. Inside. All the time. She bent over and Vic pushed deep into her. Knowing that I was watching them, she turned and looked at me. "He's so big and I'm so high," she said, "and I don't even need to be here; I'm not sick like you and the others." She moaned. Water dripped off her nipples as her body swayed back and forth to the passionate rhythm. I looked away and thought about punching myself in the dick.

Then someone in group spoke and cried, and I came back to the present. I was in a room with junkies and drunks and some poor little rich girl with big perky breasts, perfect teeth, and a perfect tan who accidentally got strung out because she didn't know painkillers were addictive. I hated her so much. I imagined I would tell her how much I hated her while I pounded her from behind, on her bedroom floor, after lights out. Then, after she'd broken skin by biting into her hand to stifle her screams of ecstasy while she climaxed, we'd lay in the dark together. All of my hate would evaporate, and I'd tell her how much I envied her because what had earned her a bed at the CSU wasn't really her fault but that I'd gotten myself there with a strict and singular mode of thought and action, that I'd done it on purpose, and that I was the physical manifestation of the phrase, "Heroin, it takes you where you want to go!" And where I was, was a hospital, a place where sick people go to get well, and I really wanted to get well, I was just too pissed off to know it.

My parents and my sister came to visit me. It was breakfast time, and I was eating a plate of the aforementioned shitty food when they walked in. I was happy to see them, maybe because I wasn't expecting them, or maybe because I was so fucking depressed and lonely, or maybe I was just glad because they're my family and I loved them, and I knew they cared about me. We talked about this or that and then they left, and I was lonely and depressed again, surrounded by drunks and junkies just like me.

On the junkie, drunky floor, there was one phone for everyone to share. One day I called my friend Darby, with whom I'd shared many nights of drunk and drugged out wonder. I expected him to make me feel better, somehow, someway. It didn't make sense. I don't know what I wanted or needed. I remember that he seemed to want to comfort me but it's like he didn't know how, or he knew he couldn't, so he did what he could do: he listened. We talked and then my turn was over. I hung up the phone feeling more alone than ever. I went to the smoking room to have a cigarette. I smoked and wished I could jump out the window to my death but there was that stupid fucking wire mesh. It seemed like there was always something keeping me from doing what I wanted.

Untitled (#30)

I am dead

I am dead

Walking carcass

Twenty-something dead shit life

Go nowhere, be nothing, and do it with style

Give me some something

Break open again

I want to hold her

I want to escape into her joy

But it's lost and I'm just getting old

Summer, 1998

THrEEe-Oh₃₀ (Same fucking season, 1998)

A few days later, my mom picked me up from the stabilization unit. I don't remember leaving the hospital, but I remember the ride home. Mom gently let me know I would be attending an outpatient rehab and that she would take me and pick me up. I would no longer be driving myself because I couldn't be trusted. And it started the next day. I agreed that I needed to go and that it would be good for me, even though deep inside I just wanted to drive straight to the West End, not to any fucking rehab. Staring out the window at passing traffic, I wondered where Betty Ann was. She hadn't come to see me in the hospital. Was it because I hadn't put her on the visitor's list? Was there a visitor's list? Maybe it was because she'd had it and she didn't want to come to see me? A person can only take so much, even a wonderful person who is loving and patient and kind. We can only ask so much of them, or give them so much before they have to let go so we don't bring them down with us. And I don't even think they really want to let go, it's just that we don't give them a choice.

                    `After a weekend retreat` at the Ridgeview Institute, my post-O.D. hospitalization and a subsequent stay at the Crisis Stabilization Spa, this would be my first foray into outpatient treatment. Day treatment rehab was a county-run program that, oddly, was housed in the lower level of a building in Marietta where I'd had a job as a telemarketer two years earlier. I'd worked there with my friend Doug. We'd get stoned and then go call people and try to convince them they needed to buy family portrait packages. I never convinced anyone, though. A man once cussed me out and told me he was going to "come down there and whoop my ass". There was this one guy who worked there who was possibly the smoothest fucker I'd ever met. He was sleazy in that way that appears sincere, but you know deep down he's only acting that way because he wants something from you. That guy sold the shit out of some family portraits. He was the pride of the telemarketing company. As I once sat at my cubicle, listening to this guy smooth talk another someone into buying portraits, observing his clean hair and flawless skin, I thought to myself, *I bet that dude gets laid like crazy.* I'd quit that job when it was time for the Joe Christmas spring tour. And now here I was, back in the same fucking building, because I'd gotten all junked out and fucked myself by almost dying. Fuck, what an inconvenience!

If I'd been making a movie, as far as independent cinema dramatic film stereotypes go, the group at this day treatment rehab would have made an excellent ensemble cast. There was Lynn, the lovable grandma whose grandchildren had forced her into rehab because she drank a bottle of wine every night before bed. But it was only *one* bottle, and she was old, so why couldn't they leave her alone? But, she was a good grandma and a sweet lady, so she went to the rehab because her grandkids asked her to. She was always kind. I bummed Camel straights off her a couple of times.

There was the earnest landscaper guy whose drinking cost him his marriage and most of his business and who truly, desperately, sincerely wanted to get sober and stay that way. There was the wheelchair tragedy guy, who got mugged when he was walking from his car to see R.E.M. play at the Omni. He didn't even make it to the show, and the shooting had left him paralyzed from the waist down. He seemed to be angry every second of every day. My heart broke for him. It amazed me he even bothered to get out of bed.

There was an elderly, blind African American man who was a recovering crack addict. I always wondered if being blind made it more difficult to smoke crack. I wondered if he had secret visions behind his blind eyes when he was high. He was vulgar and funny, and I wondered why he was there, at that rehab. Was it someone else's idea, like a judge or a concerned family member, or was it his decision?

There was the mandatory girl who was cute, quirky, intelligent, privileged, and troubled. Of course, I wanted to sleep with her. Of course, I tried. Of course, I didn't get to. It was close though. I even got to go to her house and sit on her bed and play with needles with her.

And then there was Gene, lovely and horrible and unforgettable Gene, the only person I ever met who had a permanent scar from shooting dope in the same spot so many times.

Gene was a gigantic, hulking dude. I'm six three, and he towered over me. He wore massive sneakers on huge feet to carry his exceptional height and girth. His faraway eyes lurked inside gray, sunken sockets topped with dark, bushy brows. His face was round and usually wore a scowl. Gene hated rehab. He thought it was bullshit. He hated all the counselors because they were full of shit just like his mom and dad and everyone else in the whole goddamn fucking world. I liked Gene. We talked. We got along. One day I told Gene about how I hated rehab too and that, fuck no I didn't want to be sober. That's when he told me about his connection down at the corner of MLK and Ashby. I didn't know it then, but that conversation and the information it contained would spread like a disease that would eventually kill three of my friends while completely ruining the life of another. But back then I didn't care about those kinds of possibilities; I only had one concern.

Gene knew where to score bags of dope for ten bucks a piece and I'd been paying twenty, and he said it was good shit too- really, really good shit. He was in tight with several of the dealers because he was a regular. His mom had wanted him to get clean, so he'd let her stick him in rehab even though he didn't really give a fuck. I saw her once when we went to his house to pick up his tools. Watching us leave, she had tears in her eyes. He was still her baby boy. Where had she gone wrong? What else could she do? I waved bye to her from the driver's seat. She did nothing but stare at Gene as if she might never see him again.

      Excitement pulsed through me when Gene told me about his connection. I couldn't wait to get down there. I called my friend Dex that afternoon. He said he could drive us. The next day I lied to my parents and told them I was going to Gene's house to play music after rehab. They told me to be home before dinner. I said I would and by five o'clock that afternoon I was parked on some dead-end street in the West End with a needle in my arm, watching the train fly by, smiling wide and floating away into the ether.

(Welcome to BLANK PAGE scenic byway! Please pause here for reflection)

Part IV

Be Slow on Your

Heels and

Follow the Worms

Untitled (#31)

A needle is a more familiar instrument than a guitar

My fragile fingers give way to wanting veins

I want these things all the time

I want to be downtown

I want to live

I'm sick

I'm tired of dying

Fall, 1998

Th3rty-1 (fall, 1998)

Day treatment rehab took place from eight a.m. to three p.m., Monday through Friday. At some point, I had manipulated my parents into giving me back my car and convincing them they could trust me to drive to rehab and back home again without making any detours to any drug dealers. Rehab was a good cover too because it made them think I was trying when I was only playing along. As often as I could, I made up an excuse about why I would be home a little later, and by 3:15 I'd be on I-20 east headed straight for MLK and Ashby. But it was fall, and I was a druggie. What else could they have expected me to do?

Fall is my favorite time of year. Fall is beautiful in Georgia, more beautiful than anywhere else in the world especially when you have a needle in your arm. For example, there's nothing like the warm orange glow of a fall sunset in Georgia, whether you're high out of your mind in the back seat of your friend's '78 Buick or nodding off in the front seat of your own car while you sit alone in the local cemetery with only the ducks by the lake keeping you company.

      I don't remember how long I bothered to keep attending the day treatment but, inevitably; I quit going. My parents -who may have given up- didn't press the issue. Once again, I was free, and my days were my own. I would spend them wisely, making the most of my time, honing my craft of addiction.

      Every day was the same but sometimes with different people. Time passed and Gene disappeared. I didn't see him for over a year. Maybe he went back to jail or found some new source of transportation, I can't remember. Then I was always with my friend Max. Max shared an apartment with his mom, one town over from me. His mom once said either we were gay lovers, or we were on drugs. She was right about one of those. Maybe that's why she always gave me those mistrustful looks. *What are you doing to, or with, my son?* I imagined her wondering while looking into my glazed over eyes. *No, ma'am, I did not just shoot up in your son's bathroom with the needle and dope we bought with money we pilfered from your checking account that Max got because he took your ATM card from your purse while you were asleep. We would never do anything like that!* I'd respond.

But we did. I learned so much from Max, like how to steal and return merchandise for cash from the big department stores, and just how many stolen goods you can hide in baggy pants, and that if you feel at least a modicum of remorse, it's acceptable to steal from your parents -in the long run, they'll understand, and moral qualms can often be a real hindrance. As an active addict, it's important to take note and learn from those with more experience. Those tidbits of advice and helpful hints can really get you through on the days when you have to go it alone. Remember: A teachable addict is a successful addict!

I remember the night Max told me he had his mom's ATM card. He only got out enough cash to get us each two bags of dope. He said he didn't want to take too much because he thought if he only took a little out she wouldn't notice. I was so pissed. I wanted more. I wanted him to fucking clean out the bank and buy out the goddamned dealers. But, I took a deep breath, came back to my senses, and gave thanks for what we could get. Two bags would be good for that night.

Most of the time, I could wait to shoot until I was in a comfortable spot, preferably my room or the room of a friend. Most of my using buddies were the same way. Max was the only person I ever knew who would shoot it as soon as he got it. On the night with the ATM adventure, he fixed up and got high while we were on the way home. I couldn't believe it. We were in the car; it was dark, and how did he know he even hit a vein? Then his head fell back against the seat rest and he let out a content sigh. I guessed he was a real pro.

We made it back to Mableton or Austell or wherever we went, and I shot my dope and lo, I got high as fuck. And, just like Hadley and her two friends had brought the bad news of the heroin to all the Mableton kids, I fucking told all my friends about this new hook up. And so, it was that the bad news spread throughout the kingdom and lo, all the kids got high as fuck.

During this time, my friend Elliot spent time earnestly trying to convince me to get off the shit. (He didn't understand that you don't just tell a heroin user to "quit") I could see the sincerity bleeding from his eyes, and part of me knew he was right, but the other part that ruled my life told me he didn't know shit, that everything was fine, and that dope was awesome and he was a fucking idiot. Several days after one of our late-night talks -during which he drank a box of white wine and I tried to listen in between nods- I saw Elliot at the intersection of Pisgah and South Gordon. He was in the back seat of Max's '78 Buick. His eyes had that certain glazed look, his face was red, and he had that special grin you can only get from a certain thing. He was higher than shit, and I knew it.

I can't believe it- He did it! I thought to myself. *After all that bitching and whining and telling me how I needed to quit, he fucking went off and did dope himself!*

That day began a most inglorious on-again-off-again relationship between Elliot and heroin that would last for years and eventually leave him alone and dead on his mother's living room floor.

I sat in my car, waiting for the light to turn. I looked at the person next to me, whoever that was, and then back to Max and Elliot and whoever else was in the car with them. Max nodded and smiled –he knew exactly where we were going. He smiled and waved; his droopy, doped-out eyes seemed to look straight into me. Oddly, this is one of my favorite and most vivid memories of Max. I would go on to see him less and less as the years passed, until one day I wouldn't see him at all. Then I would learn that on a Thanksgiving Eve twenty years after that day at the intersection of Pisgah and South Gordon, he got into a game of car versus pedestrian while trying to cross a major road. The car won. When I heard the news I thought of his mother and the night she asked me if Max and I were on drugs and how –high as fuck at that very moment- I'd laughed inside and lied to her face: *No mam, of course we're not on drugs*. I wondered if Max was fucked up the night he got hit. I hope he was. Then it might have hurt less.

The late afternoon sun shimmered and bounced off the clean surface of Max's car. The light changed, and it was our turn to go. We waved a fond farewell to our friends, turned through the intersection, and headed off toward the West End.

Untitled (#32)

I was a sucker

For the smile you put on my face

Happiness -painted on in warm, glowing tones.

I fell under the needle

This surgery for fools

You will be a lovely dream

And one day when you are walking

I will follow behind

With sentimental excuses

Spilling from my lips

Fall, 1998

THirTy-2 (Fall, 1998, cont.)

By the time I met Krista, the leaves were changing colors. I'd kind of known of her through some friends from school and drug house hang-outs and one time I saw her at a show, but I hadn't ever formally met her. One day we were both at our weed dealer's house and I told her I liked some poetry of her's that I'd read. I knew I was manipulating her, but I wanted to sleep with her, so I rationalized that it was okay and then convinced myself that I really, truly liked her -and her poems, which was pretty much true because she is a good writer- so I wouldn't feel bad. Later, I would also tell myself that I truly cared and that I wanted to be with her instead of just being on her and inside her and then that would make it easier on my conscience.

Several weeks later, we were alone at her house and everything was going according to plan. The first time didn't last that long. We left a stain on her parent's powder blue bed sheet. We embraced for a moment and then I was leaving. I passed her mom on my way out of the neighborhood. She was driving home from work. I tried not to look her in the eye, but I did anyway. I smiled and waved. She didn't smile or wave back.

I went home, changed clothes, and went to work at the restaurant. I felt dead inside again. Having sex with Krista hadn't helped like I'd hoped it would. I felt split open and spilled out. I wanted to scream and shove my head into the deep fryer. I'd wanted sleeping with her to take the pain away and fill up the empty spot inside and hopefully mean something but instead, it only dug the hole deeper. I knew I was using another human being to pull me out of my misery and I knew I would keep doing it and it felt like I had no power to stop it. Then the hatred set in. I wondered why I was doing the same shit over and over. I went out the kitchen's back door and lit a smoke. I watched the beautiful southern sunset blaze across the fall sky and felt sorrow cascade down on me. Here I was, my favorite time of day in my most beloved season of the year, and I could only watch this sunset for as long as my cigarette kept burning, then it was back inside to get yelled at and told to work faster and the evening would turn into night and there would be more yelling and stress and I'd somehow push through it without stabbing myself or anyone else and then it would be over and hopefully I could fuck myself up out of my mind so I wouldn't have to think or feel or be until the sun rose again and my eyes creaked open to another miserable, pointless day. And then it would happen all over again because it was only Tuesday, and I had a shift every night that week.

Untitled (#33)

Walk forward or sideways, what's the fucking difference?

Your feet end up with blisters either way

People are laughing as you search for medicine

To swallow the infection of your sores

Fall, 1998

THiRTeee-333 (fall, 1998)

It was near the middle of October when my friend Josh asked me if I'd like to join his band, playing keyboard for them on their upcoming fall tour. He'd wanted to add keys to their sound and thought I might be the guy to do it. He knew about my issues with liquids and substances, though, so maybe he was also trying to help me out. Maybe it was just one of those things you do without thinking too much about it. Who knows? For whatever reason, I loved his band, so I jumped at the chance. I saw it as an opportunity to make music with my good friends, and I saw it as my salvation- because they were a Christian Metal band, and they probably had the answers to life and happiness, and going on tour with them would fix all my problems, even though I failed to recall that going back to church had not cured me before. I knew it would work this time though. Christian metal would save my soul! I would get clean and straighten up and start a new musical career and be a good dad and reinvent myself and be the person I always knew I could be! Yeah! So, I put in my two-week notice at the Steakhouse and learned the songs. The tour was starting on Halloween night. I had to learn fast; I had a long way to go.

On the eve of the tour, I shot some dope and picked up Krista. We went to hang out and party at a friend's house with Krista's older sister and her boyfriend. As we left the trailer that Krista shared with her mother and step-father, I noticed a forlorn look on her mother's face. In the car a few minutes later, I asked Krista if she'd noticed the way her mom had been looking at us. She said she had noticed, and that her mom was probably looking at us that way because she knew we were gonna fuck.

I nodded in silence, feeling discomfort grow inside me. I didn't like the way Krista used the word 'fuck'. Then I wondered if I really liked her and, in an instant, I knew I didn't. Clarity punched me fast in the face and everything about that night and what I was doing felt wrong. But I wanted to be with someone, to feel warmth and skin and sex, and to call it love even when I knew it wasn't. I wanted someone to take the pain away,

Krista was there, and I felt powerless to stop what I'd set into motion. So, I kept driving, we arrived at some empty house somewhere, we got fucked up, and things went the way you'd think they would go.

The next morning played out like a scene from some awful 80s movie wherein I was acting as one of the central protagonists. I moved the action forward by sliding off the bed and getting dressed. No sweet, romantic cuddles- it was time to get ready to leave for tour.

I was putting on my ratty old sneakers when I realized that Krista was awake and looking at me. I told her I had to go because I was already running behind. She sat up and held the single white sheet over her breasts. There was a longing look in her eyes that asked me why I was leaving in such a hurry, and why couldn't I hold her while she woke up in my arms. Maybe I imagined that last bit, but she did look distressed. I don't remember what I said or if I even kissed her goodbye, but I remember that when I left the room, I turned back once, and she was still looking at me with that same sad look on her face.

I left the house without another word to Krista or anyone else. I knew I needed to get some dope before I had to meet up with the band later that afternoon.

I believed in the ritual of goodbye, or at least that was my excuse. Since I was going on a Christian tour to get clean and sober and get my shit together, so I could come home and tell everyone, "Hey, look at me, I'm a real, functioning person now!", I had to have that last fix, that last glorious hit, which would bring a proper end to a beautiful and terrible era.

I don't remember going to get the dope or shooting it, but I do remember being high. I said a goodbye to my parents, who were in their usual spot in the back room watching TV. Mom told me she hoped I'd find what I was looking for. I don't recall my dad saying anything although he probably mumbled something; he usually did. Then I was at the show. It was in a church gym. It seemed crowded. I was glad I was high, although it was wearing off, I was holding on to every bit of the sensation I could. That and a weird orange glow is all I remember of the show. The next day found me sitting in the back of the tour van, wrapped in that same quilt that my grandmother had made, shivering, pissed off, and hating everyone around me. I wasn't hating them because I was coming off the shit; I hated them because they looked happy and free and that's how I wanted to be but I wasn't, so I held it against anyone who was. I used to joke and say "happy people should be shot on sight". Maybe, secretly, I wasn't kidding.

Josh's band was called World Against World. We were going out as the support act for Squad Five-O, a Christian ska-core band that would later morph into a regular 'ole non-denominational rock-and-roll band. I'd been a fan of World Against World since they'd been the crusty punk band Spudgun, and, although I wasn't in the best place or the clearest frame of mind, I was sincerely happy to be going out on the road with them. Now they were a little older and a lot angrier and they dressed in all black and played atonal hyper sludge crust that leaned more towards black metal than punk rock. As I mentioned, they assigned me the role of adding keys to their sound. I kept the 1980s Casio keyboard set on the pipe organ voice and did my best Cradle of Filth impersonation to fill in the melody gaps in the massive wall of crusty black dirge.

For thirty days that November we trekked across the Southeast, over into the Midwest, and back again, playing a mix of churches and all ages venues. We played the Christian club in Little Rock, Arkansas where Evanescence played their first gigs. We played a church basement gig in Kansas City Missouri. There was an awesome pipe organ in the sanctuary I played while Squad Five-O was doing their soundcheck. We played an all-ages venue in Baltimore that had a WWE style wrestling training center in the basement with a real ring and everything. I met a super-hot girl there. We hung out in the parking lot, chain-smoking and talking about this and that. It was nice to feel like I could relate to someone for a minute. The venue used to be a restaurant. There was a long prayer session in the kitchen. It was cold, and I wondered when the praying would end.

There was a show in Florida at an all-ages venue where I had a heartfelt talk with my friend Jason. We sat in the van. I broke down crying. He prayed for me with his hand on my shoulder. I wished that, at that moment, I would be magically healed, and my life would suddenly be awesome. I tried so hard to believe, to make it happen, but it didn't. I still felt like shit, but I was thankful that Jason was my friend. I knew these guys cared about me. I knew they were trying to help me, and it broke my heart because, deep down, I knew they couldn't.

The last show of the tour was at a record store on the beach, somewhere in South Carolina. I was so depressed that I could barely pretend to have a good time. I'd gotten through the dope withdrawal, which wasn't as bad as I'd expected it to be, I'd gone thirty days with only cigarettes and coffee to comfort me (the guys always steered me away from the beer coolers at the truck stops and gas stations), and I was still alive, although not happy to be so. I knew the next day I'd be back in Mableton, just a short drive from MLK and Ashby, and I was fucking scared out of my mind.

Untitled (#34)

Bruises don't ask for help

They only feed

A needle became my friend

Quotes in red couldn't heal my fucked-up heart

Ten-dollar salvation

My cup runneth over

I slip away into a cigarette laced daydream

Fall, 1998

ThIRTeee-4 (fall, 1998)

It was already dark when Josh and Ryan dropped me off at home. My red car was in its parking spot, the security lights made halos at the carport's edge, yellow and orange and red leaves outlined the driveway. I told them I'd had an awesome time, thanked them for taking me along, and went inside. I don't remember who was there or if they were up or anything at all. I was so unhappy to be home I went straight to bed and wished to never wake up.

The next day the phone rang early. It was Krista. She was upset. She wanted to know why I hadn't called her at all during the last two weeks of the tour. I gave her some bullshit excuse about not having the money or a phone card or something.

There was a pause.

I held my breath.

She told me she was pregnant.

Even though I almost felt like I knew what was coming, the words still slashed my soul to pieces. My ears rang so loud I couldn't hear my thoughts. I trembled and slumped down into the gossip seat. I think I stopped breathing. Krista's voice was a distant whisper. She asked if I was still there. I said I was although I wasn't sure. Could there possibly be some mistake? Was she sure? No, there was no mistake; there had been no one else, just me. She was sure. I think the floor disappeared, and I saw myself floating over a bottomless pit of hell.

I launched into a profusion of apologies and expressions of regret. I told her I was sorry for ruining her life. I told her I felt like her whole family must totally hate me for what I'd done.

She told me I hadn't ruined anyone's life and that no one hated me. I wondered why she was being nice to me. It was confusing. I wanted to be hated and scorned and reviled. That would have been easy. But to be spoken to in such a soft and understanding way was painful and baffling and why couldn't I have just taken her home that one night instead of insisting on the park and the blanket and the dark? Maybe it was the pills and the rum that took us there. Maybe that was the night that was the cause of this current conversation. Maybe, but it could have been another, or the other, or the one before or after that.

      We talked, but I don't know how the rest of the conversation went. What I remember is going straight to the West End the next morning, shocked that I'd made it through the previous day without getting high or killing myself. I scored three bags and headed back toward home. But I couldn't wait. The drive was too long. Besides, this was a special circumstance, I needed some immediate relief. So much for sobriety….

      I took the Six Flags exit off I-20 West and stopped at the little gas station just off the exit. I tried to look inconspicuous as a searched the parking lot for a soda can. My eyes spotted a can on a bed of leaves in the curb's corner. I grabbed it and tossed it in the car. Then I went into the store and bought a small bottle of water. I had plenty of cigarettes, and I'd brought a rig with me, so now all I needed was a comfortable spot. It was a Sunday morning and with no one at work I found solitude in a nearby unfinished neighborhood. I parked at the top of a hill and looked out over the empty house frames, skeletons for future families with their future fights and future disappointments. I flipped the soda can over and wiped the concave bottom out with the tail of my t-shirt. It wasn't my trusty spoon, but it would do. I emptied the bags of dope out onto the can, added the water, stirred, drew it up into the needle, and drove it home. I leaned back and sighed. I could breathe again. I could figure out what to do. It would be okay. My heavy eyelids flapped loud and slow and my warm body sank into the seat. And the world was right once again.

   After I'd settled into the high, I drove to Krista's house. I wanted to see her and comfort her and let her know I was there for her. I couldn't believe I'd gotten another woman pregnant. I'd done the same thing again. And we'd been careful and used protection except when we didn't. But this time would be different! I floated to Krista's in my red hovercraft car, resolving to do the right thing, what I should have done with Betty Ann. I would stay with her. I'd ask her to marry me and we'd raise the kid together. No bitching, no complaining, no avoiding, just face it and be responsible and try to be happy. I told myself to be positive, and that everything would work out and that it really wasn't that bad, for real. I was high as fuck.

I got to Krista's. We talked. I explained my intentions. She asked me if I was still shooting dope. To be real and honest, I told her I was, and that, in fact, I was high at that exact moment. I could feel the loathing and disappointment oozing from her pores. I don't remember the rest of the conversation. Some time passed, and I was coming down. I had to do something about that.

The next thing I remember is being high, sitting on the curb in front the tattoo shop that my friend Jason's dad owned. I don't know what day it was or how much time had passed. I'd spoken with Krista sometime earlier, maybe that day or the day before, and she'd told me I wasn't allowed to come to her house anymore and to not call her either. There wasn't any discussion -that's how it would be. But what about my good intentions; what about doing the right thing? Apparently, all my chances to do the right thing had been used up, and my good intentions weren't good enough. Nine months later my second son was born. They never allowed me to meet him, which made sense to me: It's good for parents to protect their children from bad people.

Untitled (#35)

Jesus Christ, bastard son of the Most High

Illegitimate

Born to a world

To be hated, rejected, killed for loving

Spited bastard cum wad

How loose would the cunt be that takes in the cock of the Most High?

The Lord sayeth, "Art thou not satisfied?"

Mary replies, "Give me now a cigarette from thy bosom."

The cock of the Most High fucks all over the world

All the Marys are bleeding

Their soft virgin cunts are ripped open

And God is cumming all over their smiling whore faces

They're sitting in the confession booths

Waiting to get fucked all over again

Their faces twist with glee

The words of the Most High tickle their ears

Let the virgins conceive

She bled for Jesus

With her legs spread, she was pounded

The cock of the Lord brought pain and sad wishes

To a girl who only wanted a friend,

Just got fucked in the end

Fall/winter, 1998

ThIRty35 (winter, 1998)

After learning about Krista's pregnancy, I walked up to The Deep End and looked down into its swirling mass of shit, hate, and fear, and I dove in headfirst, even though I knew I couldn't swim in such dark, turbulent waters. My outlook on life went from "it's not so bad, I'm gonna make it" to "fuck everything and everyone- let's see how bad this can really get."

Josh, Jason, and Ryan, my pals in World Against World, noticed that the rehab tour hadn't really taken. They called a band meeting and told me I had a choice: do drugs or be in the band, but I couldn't do both. It didn't take them that long to find a new keyboard player.

To legitimately support my habit, I got a new job washing dishes at a local Italian restaurant. I spent every cent I made on dope, booze, and cigarettes. The afternoon I was filling out my application I saw Krista and her mom having lunch there. I said hello. I asked her if she was still pregnant. She said she was. She asked me if I was still on drugs. I looked her in the eye and lied, telling her I was sober and then mumbling something involving the phrase "One day at a time".

I felt her looking deep into me and through me. She knew I was full of shit.

That was the last time Krista and I ever spoke in person. About five years later she would call me and ask if I'd be willing to sign papers, so the nice guy she'd married could become the child's legal father. I thought her request was odd because I'd never signed a birth certificate, but I said that, of course, I would do whatever she needed me to. She never sent the papers, and I never heard from her again. But, over the years people have told me she's doing great and has a large family, a loving husband, and a wonderful life. That makes me smile. Even though I treated her horribly, it seems vain and stupid of me to think I could've ruined her life. I wasn't ruining anyone's life but my own.

Around this time, I would wake up and drive into the West End to get my dope first thing in the morning. My friend Max said shooting up right after you rub the sleep from your eyes was a glorious thing. It's kind of like waking and baking, but, you know, this was heroin, not weed. I thought back to when, a couple of years earlier, I had started smoking weed first thing in the morning, right before I'd have my morning coffee and cigarettes. At that time, I felt like I'd crossed a line. Now I was about to cross another line, a different kind of line, one that it turned out, is much harder to come back from once it has been crossed. But I stepped over it, anyway. What did I care, my life was over, so fuck it. Fuck me, and fuck everything. And so it was- totally fucked.

As it turned out, Max was right. Starting your day with a shot of dope was a wonderful thing but a terrible thing as well. But bad ideas are usually a lot of fun, at least for a while, until you come down and you wonder what the fuck you were supposed to do with the rest of your day. This was a microcosmic version of my life at the time; every day, every time I'd come down, I'd wonder what I was supposed to do, or what I could do, or whatever. I never knew. Everything was a circular chase from nothing into nowhere. Soon my answer would come. It didn't take long before my entire life revolved around getting and using heroin. I'd reached a new level. I was in a new place. I looked around and it looked like shit.

The weather was stark and cold. It was winter. The dreaded holiday season had come and gone, and I didn't remember it at all. The weather seemed to grow colder every day. I was always cold, inside and out. I spent lots of time at a friend's house. He used to heat the small home by cranking his oven on high heat and leaving the door open. I used to like to sit down on the kitchen floor and shoot up right there in front of the oven. I'd often spend the night. I'd get holed up in a cozy space and not want to leave. I felt like I was in a dope cocoon on the couch, glued to the cushions in front of a space heater, an Enya CD playing on repeat. Everything was perfect and comfy and beautiful until the sun rose and the harsh day shattered my illusions. Then it was time to get more dope. A cigarette and a couple cups of coffee would get me out the door. I'd usually be back by the afternoon but some days it took longer to get money together and score. But, I also hung out at other houses and with other people and it seemed like we were all shuffling back and forth with only one intention and that was the only thing that kept us going.

Untitled (#36)

I can hear the echo in your voice

Time melts into a spoon

Watery eyes, backyard winter night

Cold wind bounces off medicated skin

We walk in time to the rhythm of the city

Waiting is always the worst part

When will the man come down from the porch?

Holes in his sweater, holes in his teeth

Mother is watching from the window

Peeking out onto the waiting customers

It's not our neighborhood

It's not my life anymore

Living to a certainty –choice

A longing to feel more

A broken will

Exaggeration is the truth

Watch us all failing each other

You're stitching up the pain with emptiness

Wanting —a place in the sun, a needle, and a son

The pale shades wash away in a blur and taint this purity of experience

Time weaves thoughts into secrets that shine from ultra-fine scars

Leaving memories on our arms

You left memories on my heart

Winter, 1998

Th3rtEe-6 (winter, 1998)

Sometime near the middle or end of December, I came to accept the absolute, undeniable reality that I was no longer having any fun, ever, that getting high was becoming an effort to maintain normalcy, and that I fucking hated myself and my life. I was cracking. This was it. I knew I was done. I had to be done, or I'd be dead. I told my parents I wanted to go stay with my grandma and get clean. I had myself convinced that this would work, that I didn't need professional help, that I could do this on my own. I don't know why they listened, but they did. Back then I was still delusional enough to believe love and family and determination were enough.

So, I sat in the passenger seat, mumbling and nodding off, high out of my mind, with my mother driving me to her mother's house in the country so I could be away from everything and everyone, so I could come off the shit, so I could change my life. And I was ready. I was ready to get sober and be a good guy and a dad and do all the right things. I knew it. That's why I had six bags of dope and two clean needles hidden in the inner lining of my shaving kit.

Untitled (#37)

Wrap up a smile

Trade with me

Let me **bleed out** all excuses

And come to the honest decision to change

Self-esteem is archived

Shut up in a glass case in a cold, stiff museum

I look and think, "I wish I owned that work of art"

Winter, 1998

TheeerTeE-

7 (Winter, end of 1998)

I love the Alabama countryside where my grandma lives. Her house sits along a lone strip of two-lane blacktop, in between somewhere and nowhere, surrounded by beautiful nature and hillbilly ruin. I'd always loved it there, even when I was an ungrateful, complaining teenager who despaired at the area's lack of modernity. The land breathed redemption and possibility and isolation, and I wanted all of those. I had enough dope to last for a day and a half or, maybe two. After that, I'd be hurting, and I knew it. Then my optimistic mindset might fade away. Then what would I do? I did not understand what I was heading into or what I would do when I got there. This wasn't like before when I had that short stretch of forced sobriety due to being in the hospital and all that. My using hadn't been as consistent at that point but by this time I'd become a daily user. It scared me, but I tried not to take it to heart. I was just going to quit and that would be that and afterward I'd just drink beer and smoke weed and get on with my life as any other normal person would. I had to get through this one little patch. I had to get fixed up and then I could get back to my life. Then I'd be okay. Yes, then I'd be just fine.

I'm sure that my parents must have told my grandma why I was there and why I'd asked to stay with her. She welcomed me into her home like I was there for any old visit. She didn't ask any questions except was I hungry or did I want something to drink. Since she didn't ask, I didn't tell her I was trying to stay in my comfort zone and avoid another hospital or trauma center or rehab facility. I never said I wasn't truly committing to living a new, sober life, and that I was just trying to find a middle space with no commitment that didn't hurt too bad or ask too much so I could give as little as possible and still get away without too many scrapes or bruises.

She helped me get set up in the second bedroom. It was the one closest to the main room. I always stayed in this room as a kid, my head sunken into a feather pillow, listening to the trucks pass by on the highway. Grandma always left the closet light on for me. The warm orange glow comforted me and kept the monsters away. I turned it on that night. It still glowed the same way it always did. But now there were too many monsters, and they weren't afraid of the light.

Since I was already high when I arrived, I gritted my teeth and save my dope for the next day. That night, after grandma had gone to bed, as I laid out my tools on the toilet seat in the backroom bathroom, I felt a twinge of guilt knowing I was about to shoot up drugs in my grandmother's home. Then the needle was in my arm and I didn't feel guilty about much of anything at all.

I coasted through the next day on autopilot, waiting for night to fall, for the house to be quiet, and for grandma to be asleep. Then I was in the back bathroom again, a warm glow coursing through my veins, caressing me, making me whole. I sighed- that was the last of my dope. I flushed the tiny plastic bags, went to my room, and listened to my Enya cassette in the dark. I was a Shepard Moon. I'd told myself that I would get high one last time, and that I would have a special, ceremonial goodbye. I'd imagined myself at peace, letting go of my dope habit, and feeling happy as I embraced my new life. But as I sat alone in the dark, staring into the flame of the single candle, all I could feel was emptiness and fear. What was I going to do without heroin? Who would protect me from life and the world? Who was I going to turn to when everything was cold and harsh and bearing down on me, threatening to crush me into dust? What was I going to do without it? I sighed and lit a cigarette and gave up on thinking. I'd just have to wait and see. I inhaled deep and felt the warm pulse surge through me. I stared into the flame and let the high carry me away.

The sickness came sooner than I'd expected. It felt like the worst flu I'd ever had in my life, times one hundred. I kept trying to stretch my legs, but they kept shrinking back in. I couldn't stop shaking. I was sweating and freezing. My back was stiff, and I felt like I'd been the guest of honor at a hammer party. *Wow, this is really happening,* I mused to myself, *I'm actually dope-sick. Just like in the movies!* As naïve as it sounds, in the back of my mind, I wasn't expecting to get really, truly sick. I thought I'd just quit, and that it might be kind of uncomfortable. Although it could've been worse, this was worse than I'd expected.

I was lying on the living room couch. Grandma had the TV on. I tried to stare at the screen, but my eyes kept watering and obscuring my vision. My aunt and uncle came over that afternoon. My uncle cracked a joke that made me think he was subtly saying, "Yep, this is what you get, you little shit." Maybe that's not what he meant, though. I felt like offering a retort, but my mouth-word-talky-brain mechanism wasn't working. I looked up at them and let out a pathetic, monosyllabic reply. I think they grinned at me. By then the entire family knew why I was there. In previous attempts at relocation strategies, I'd spilled my guts to various family members, telling them what was going on, begging them to let me come to stay with them so I could escape the "bad influences" around me in Mableton and "clean up". Overwhelmed with embarrassment, this infuriated my father. Guess he couldn't take knowing everyone knew what a fuck-up his only son was.

    I stayed on the couch all day, only getting up to smoke, wrapped in a quilt, shaking so much I could barely bring the cigarette to my lips. At some point that day I sat in a scalding bath to warm up. While I sat shivering in the tub, I remembered taking baths in that same tub when I was a child. I remembered the joy of splashing around and then drying off in front of the old gas-powered wall heater that would sputter with its blue and orange flames. I looked at my skinny arms and wished I could cry, but I couldn't, I was too empty for any tears to come. That night I woke up drenched in sweat. I must have made a racket because my grandma came into the room to see if I was alright. She helped me put fresh, dry sheets on the bed. And she helped me change the sheets the next night, and the night after that as well.

A few days passed and I felt like I had a shitty cold instead of the flu. My body was still sore. I felt exhausted and limp. My grandma encouraged me to go out into the sun. It was a freezing mid-morning in January when I walked out into the backyard for the first time since I'd gotten there. The rays of the Piedmont sun covered me in their glow. I pulled my housecoat tight around my body, groaned with ungrateful displeasure at the bright orb, and shuffled over to the swing and sat down. I lit a smoke and stared off into the Alabama countryside. And once again, I wished I was dead.

Untitled (#38)

Of all the people I know, I hate myself the most

Tragedy's sister pays a visit

I offer her an embarrassment

If you like you

Then fuck you

Fuck you and every happy fuck

Walk your own two feet into hell

Join me

I'm waiting

Winter, 1999

ThIrTy-H8tE
(winter, 1999)

A few more days had gone by and I had become more mobile. It was then that my family members tried to nudge me into various activities. This fucking pissed me off. I wanted them to leave me alone so I could brood and wallow in my self-pity and depression. But they would have none of it. Grandma was always smiling at me, cracking odd jokes, complimenting me, and encouraging me to be positive. I put up a bratty-kid mental block. At the same time, I knew she was right. But even though I knew she was right, I would not acknowledge that, not even to myself. No one would teach me- I would teach myself, and that was that. Still, I expressed none of this outwardly to anyone. I went out in the yard with Grandma. I helped prune the plants for spring. We planted a strawberry patch. She showed me the basics of quilting. We played cards and watched teen dramas on TV, which I oddly found a great deal of comfort in. And she always had a good thing to say, and I never ceased resenting her for it, even though I was grateful at the same time.

Then there was my uncle. If my grandma was a priestess of positivity, my uncle was the pope. I still think he believes church and nature hikes can cure pretty much any ailment that a person may have, be it mental, spiritual, physical, or all the above. First, it was off to the woods to witness the beauty of the cliffs and the falls. And they were beautiful, but I kept wishing I was sitting somewhere, chain-smoking, thinking terrible thoughts. There were several of these nature trips, but I only vividly remember the one. There was also the prayer meeting, where he and several friends from church, including a recovering addict, did the laying on of hands and the praying of the prayers. Satan was renounced, they called the power of the Lord down, and I was alone in a chair in the middle of an empty room while a group of grown men chanted over me. But I tried to tune in. Maybe this will work, I thought. I gritted my teeth and searched for God. I wanted with all of my black heart to make some kind of contact. I wanted that lightning strike spiritual experience I was so sure would wash me clean and make me whole and new all in one fell swoop and then I could get back to my life thank you very much, amen. And I felt something as they prayed and hooted and hollered and banished the devil. Maybe it helped. I knew I wanted it to.

Then the night arrived when my aunt and uncle finally dragged me to the actual church. Ugh. But even so, even as I maintained my wall of indifference, I somehow tried to connect with the spirit. I knew I was sick, and I wanted to get well, I didn't know how. The congregation rose to their feet, and I listened to my uncle belt out the words of the hymn and I knew in my heart he believed every single fucking word and that his life made sense and he had direction and joy and happiness. And at that moment I envied him more than anybody in the whole goddamn world.

At some point, not too much later, I started hanging out with Brianna and Mark. They were the next-door neighbors. Brianna was my cousin twice removed. I liked it at their house. They had beer, weed, and a PlayStation with *Resident Evil 2*. And they lived just across the driveway with my other second cousin, Mae. How convenient for me. I stayed over there as much as I could; getting as fucked up as I could on cheap beer and dirt weed. But they had work and lives and all that normal stuff I didn't seem to want any part of, yet I secretly did, but I didn't or couldn't admit it. Other times I'd drink by myself in the woods, sitting next to the tiny pond where I used to play as a kid. Now I was in my early twenties, scribbling self-loathing tinged nonsense into a diary book that my best friend had given me for my birthday.

One evening I was drunk in the woods, sitting on a fallen tree that lay next to the little pond. It was getting late, and the darkness was thickening around me, drawing me in. I blinked hard and tried to focus my blurry vision. The cigarette tasted stale. The evening was cold. While focusing on the quiet, I heard the voices of my Grandmother and my cousin Mae, calling for me in the distance. I was sure they knew I had gone into the woods because I did so pretty much every day. I felt annoyed. I wanted to be alone, left to rot in the forest, but I also wanted to be saved. I wanted to be pitied and lifted up. I wanted to be pulled out of the shit I'd covered myself in. I wanted to be given a wonderful life, and I wanted to feel like I deserved that wonderful life. I listened to their voices calling for me. I could hear their fear. Everyone knew how easy it was to get lost in those woods after dark. And when it gets dark out there in the Alabama countryside, it gets fucking *dark*. I listened for a few more minutes, imagining how bad they may or may not feel. Maybe I was just irritating them because I was late for supper? But they never stopped calling for me, so I got to my feet and stumbled through the dark back to the house. I wonder what I did with the empty tall boy cans. Did I leave them out in the woods? If I did, are they still there?

I don't remember how long these kinds of nights went on. I don't remember how long I stayed there. I remember that no matter how much beer I drank alone in the woods or at my cousin's house, or how much weed I smoked, the giant gaping wound in my soul never healed and I felt no better; I only felt emptier.

My Grandma cried when I told her I was leaving to go back home. She asked me to stay with her, to take a year off and get better. I told her I couldn't. I felt like my life was speeding away without me. I told myself that I was well enough to go back, that it was time, and that I could stay clean and just drink and smoke weed, and everything would be fine, and I'd be happy, get a new band together, and be successful in no time.

So, I left.

As I rode away, sitting in the back of my sister's car, stoned out of my mind, deep in my heart I knew none of it was true and that there was only one reason I was going back to Atlanta. The small voice inside was screaming at me to ask my sister to take me back to Grandma's, to tell her I'd changed my mind, pleading with me, begging me to follow my heart. And I knew it. I wanted so badly to scream, "Turn around, I want to go back!" But I couldn't. I had to do what the drugs told me to do. So, I said nothing at all. I sat in the backseat in silence, feeling overwhelmed with anxiety and hopelessness, tears brimming in my eyes.

Untitled (#39)

Your heart paints your eyes

To keep still feet

Waiting to fly

And send her up to a heavenly cloud

And say **HELLO**

To the rest of your lives

Winter, 1999

3tHirTy N9ine

(winter, 1999)

I'd been home less than a week and I was nodding off to the sweet warm surge of the drugs in my veins. One of my first memories of that week is getting high and going to see my friends at the pizza restaurant where they all worked. It was late on a Friday night. I remember sitting at the bar talking with my friend Cal, asking if he could get me a job there in the kitchen, telling him I'd just gotten back home, and I was ready to start over and move on with my life and really get better. Then a few minutes later I was puking in the bushes out in front of the restaurant. I didn't get that job.

Two days later I was back at Grandma's. I think I stayed there for a couple more weeks before the cycle started all over again. I felt like I had ruined things between Grandma and me by leaving that first time, that I'd broken her heart and I couldn't make everything better by coming back. I'd also broken my momentum, if I'd ever really had any. And in my heart maybe I knew I couldn't stay with my grandmother and heal and get sober because I really didn't want to. I don't know why I couldn't face the pain. I never stayed still long enough to figure that out. Then, as if I'd never left, I was back in my friend's kitchen, sitting in front of the open oven, nodding off as the waves of warmth from the electrical appliance floated over me, feeling that chemical peace in my flesh, tasting the dope in the back of my mouth, not caring about anything or anyone, never ever wanting to be anywhere else in the world.

It was during these next several days, maybe when I was sprawled out on someone's floor, maybe when I was shooting dope alone in the same room where I'd spent my high school years, or maybe when I was low on money, smoking other people's weed and drinking other people's beer and I couldn't get fucked up enough to make the pain in my muscles and joints and heart and soul go away, maybe it was in one of those times when I knew for certain it was time for everything to change. I had to get out. I knew it more than I'd ever known anything. This misery was too much. It had to end, permanently.

Untitled (#40)

I'd trade in all my memories to live a moment of your life

You weave the story that everyone will forget

Your life is blind, but I see the path

I want a life to destroy

Beautiful decay and smiles that don't lie

I want a mind that I can fuck

Fuck the lights out of my eyes

I'm never getting out of this goddamn town

Winter, 1999

FouR-Oh40 (spring, 1999)

I passed some more time in a stationary pattern until one night I was hanging out at my sister's place with our friends Smiles and Mel who were in town for a short visit with Mel's mom. They'd been living in the mountains of North Carolina for a while and they were telling us about the little town of Boone while we sat on chairs and couches, pulling on joints and sipping on drinks. My skin was crawling the way it always did, and I nervously rubbed my toes together while my heart raced inside my chest. I tried to will the weed and the drinks to be heroin-strong while I listened to Mel describe the town, making it seem totally enchanting. I wanted to go to this little mountain hideaway. I ached for the relief I imagined it would bring.

Possibly using their hippie powers to read my thoughts, but more likely seeing I needed help, Smiles and Mel offered for me to come live with them, adding that they could also use some help with the rent. Feeling a burst of hope for a better future that I hadn't felt in what seemed like an eternity, I instantly said yes please, and thank you and when do we leave? Tomorrow, Smiles said. I told them I'd be ready to go in the morning, and I totally fucking meant it.

The sky was gray and spitting drizzle when I slouched out of bed the next morning. I'd already packed the night before, so I was ready to go -I just needed to score some dope to take with me before Mel and Smiles swung by to pick me up on their way out of town. I left the house as quick as I could and sped down to MLK and Ashby.

The rain had picked up by the time I hit the West End. None of the regular dealers were out. I circled the neighborhood, again and again, praying to God (literally), that I would find someone. I stopped at the dope house. No one came to the window. I got back into my mom's car which I'd borrowed, lying and telling her I needed to run up to the store. To pay for all the bad checks I'd written for dope cash, my parents had sold my little red car while I was at my Grandma's.

      I made loop after loop, peering through the rain, hoping and praying to see someone I recognized who would have what I needed. Still, my prayers went unanswered, and I never found any of the usual dealers. So, I gave up. After leaving the sprawling West End neighborhood and getting back out on one of the main roads that led out to I-20, I saw a fellow Mable Town dope fiend. He was standing on a street corner wearing a grim frown, his hands shoved deep into the pockets of his rain-soaked blue hoodie. I waved him down and pulled over, hoping he could tell me where to score, but he hadn't found anyone either. I felt my heart sink. I'd have to look into other avenues of getting wasted. I didn't feel sick, but I didn't feel good or normal, either. I said bye to my fellow fiend and went back home. Driving down 20 West, I felt relieved that I would not be doing this thing anymore. I couldn't wait to get the fuck out of town. I was going to a new place to start a new life, and, maybe for the first time, I was no longer hesitant or afraid; I was just glad.

      I knew I was leaving Betty Ann and Parker. I don't remember if I told them I was leaving. Although I thought about them most of the time, I don't know if I thought about them much at all on that day. It filled my mind with anxious horror, a black wave that seemed to crowd out nearly everything else. I knew I felt that if I stayed; I wouldn't be around much longer. I had to go. I hoped that one day they would understand. I rationalized everything. It would be better if I left because even if I stayed, I wouldn't be there, and that would have been the worst thing of all.

When I walked back into the house, my mom told me I'd missed my ride. She said Smiles and Mel had been by and had already left town because I wasn't here. Black cords wrapped around my heart and squeezed. I'd missed my chance. I was stuck again. I said nothing as I hung my head and sighed. When were they here? I finally asked. A few minutes ago, my mom replied. I cursed myself inside. And just as I was turning to slink back to my room, I heard the rumbling cadence, like a happy child blowing metal bubbles, of the VW bus heading down our driveway. They were back! The black cords loosened. I stepped outside to meet them. It turned out they'd gone to gas up the van and decided to stop by one more time just in case I'd come back. It was a miracle. I almost couldn't believe it. I'm sure I thanked them profusely while also thanking God and then I grabbed my bags, said *bye* to mom, and hopped into the van. I sat in the middle seat with my head leaning against the window and I closed my eyes as the VW burped and gurgled and pulled out onto the open road.

After we'd left the big city far behind and the sun was sinking low in the gray sky, Mel lit the fat joint she'd brought along for the journey into the Appalachian hills. This was the moment I'd been waiting for. Since I'd had a two weeks break from dope while I'd been back at Grandma's and then I'd only been using again for a couple of days or so, I was in that strange physiology which isn't quite dope sickness yet isn't normal physical wellness either. I could feel my body craving the H, but it could've been much, much worse. Still, I would do anything and everything I could to medicate myself and avoid the aches and pains I couldn't stretch or bend away. Worst of all was the bottomless emotional hole I felt inside. I had to fill it before I tripped and fell into its black abyss.

I eagerly pulled on the joint, taking in the aromatic smoke, trying to will it to be as strong as possible, trying to force it to be what it could not. I held in each toke as long as I could. The numbness from the weed blanketed me, and for a moment, I felt happy, whole, sane, warm and calm. I looked out at the headlights that sped by in the dark. I could hear my friends talking quietly in the front seats. The road hummed beneath us. And there in the van, as some jangly music played softly in the background, I hoped for my sorrow to be whisked away, and I drifted off to sleep. When I awoke we were curving up a mountain road. Suddenly afraid and filled with an inexplicable dread, I asked Mel where we were. Smiling, she reached back, patted my arm, and looked into my eyes. "Don't worry," she said, "We're almost there."

The End

And then, and then: An Afterword

I've been wondering if an afterword would be a good way to end this book, something where I say, "Hey, I did all these drugs, I drank all those drinks, I did all that bad shit and hurt all those people but now I'm okay, life is good, and everything is all better. And, if you're on drugs, you can quit, and it can be all better for you too - yay!" But, here I am at the end and I'm not sure what I want to say. I know I want to say something, but I also know I don't want to say that. That would be insincere, trite, cliché, etc, etc. Instead of making any bullshit promises or half-hearted positive proclamations, I'll write a little about what it's been like for me over the last few years and where I am now.

I entered recovery in earnest in the spring of 2007. I was thirty-one years old. Today I am forty-three. I started drinking and using when I was eighteen. It only took me three years to get from smoking cigarettes and drinking booze to shooting heroin.

It's been twelve years since the last time I shot dope.

I've been completely sober since July, 2012. From 2007 to the summer of 2012, I was never able to sustain my sobriety for more than about a year and a half at a time. Sick of relapsing, in a last-ditch-effort I went to Alcoholics Anonymous -again. It worked.

In some ways, these years of full sobriety have been the best years of my life, in other ways they have not. Some things have gotten better, some things have not.

I haven't seen Parker since his high school graduation. That was almost four years ago.

I've still never seen or met my second son in person.

I still don't know how to come to terms with being someone's dad. That is painful and confusing.

Every day I want to talk with Parker, but I can't ever seem to pick up the phone. I miss him. We usually text each other once a week or so. That's not great, but it's an improvement that I'm thankful for. My relationship with my own father remains fractured to this day. None of us called each other this past Father's Day.

I think about Betty Ann every day. I miss her every day, too. I'm not sure if we are friends or if we ever will be again. I don't know if I'll ever be able to make up for all the hurt that I caused her. I don't know if I can ever really forgive myself for what I did to her and Parker.

Today I dream of being a reliable, self-sufficient adult who knows how to live and is at peace with life and the world. But, these are just fantasies, and I am none of these things. However, I am learning, and I am grateful for that. Even though I fucked up and left my son and his mother, I have been blessed with many experiences and friendships, and I know now that regret is a futile notion that only brings pain. Yet on many days it fills me to capacity.

I still think about heroin. I wish I never did but its presence lingers as a scar on my soul that will never completely heal. When I think about dope, sometimes I feel a hot flash across my chest. That feeling scares the shit out of me. Sometimes I think I smell it on the wind, which makes my mouth water, and that also terrifies me. I guess it's just something that will always be with me. I accept that. It's okay. Even though I experience these phenomena, and have these emotional associations, I know in my heart that heroin can't hurt me anymore. I am safe. I breathe a sigh of relief when I can remember that.

Some days I still want to get bombed out of my skull, just blank out and escape into a bottle of booze or pills or whatever I can find. Then, by some miracle I don't understand I remember how awful that way of life was for me and I go escape into a good horror book, movie, or record instead.

I feel so corny saying it, but, despite everything, today I do experience a good deal of happiness and I'm beginning to learn how to be sincerely grateful for my life. And that is by choice; it's something I have to work at, or toward, every single day. Some days I fail completely and I want to open my veins up with the nearest sharp object and empty my life out on the floor. Sometimes those days all get stuck together and form a chain of hopeless weeks. Sometimes they don't. I constantly struggle against guilt and shame and all the other shit that just makes me want to give up and go bury my head in the yard. It is worth the effort, though, and I'm seeing small miracles all the time. I love and cherish my sobriety.

That's where I am today. I hope that one day I will be totally free of regrets. I hope that one day I will have a close father/son relationship with Parker and with my own dad, too. I hope that all the hurts I caused others will one day be fully healed. Lastly, I hope that this book might help someone feel better. I've been there, and, although it may not get perfect, it gets better. I used to think people who told me that were full of shit, but it turns out I was wrong. Thank you for reading this part of my story.

Love, Russell

Spring, 2019

Acknowledgements

For years I considered writing this book or something like it. If not for the following people, I probably never would have gotten it done. To my former sponsors, Hal and Erin, for helping me want to stay alive and stay sober. To Dana, for pushing me to start and then to actually finish this book. To Holly, for driving me to my first meeting, for help with proofreading and editing, and for enthusiasm, encouragement, and insight. To Trevor and John Wayne, for beta reading, encouragement, and for many kind words. To Andy at ATLATL Press, for encouragement and inspiration. To Parker, for accepting my amends and allowing me to be around. And to Betty Ann, for her blessing. Thank you all. Words can't tell you how grateful I am.

To my fellow addicts, recovering or not, who may feel that you have fucked up your life beyond repair, that you are worthless, that there is no hope. Please, please, please don't give up on yourself or your life. We can all use our pain, our shared experience, to help each other. We're all in this together.

Russell Holbrook is a writer, painter, and musician. Since 2015, his short stories have appeared in close to a dozen anthologies, including (but not limited to) *Mondo Bizarro* (Rooster Republic Press), *The Classics Never Die! An Anthology of Old-School Movie Monsters* (Red All Over Books), and the ongoing international horror/weird fiction anthology series, *Gruesome Grotesques* (Phantasmagoria Publishing). He is the co-founder and guitarist for Tooth and Nail Records artist Joe Christmas, as well as the co-founder/guitarist/keyboardist for Chapel Hill, NC's Choose Your Own Adventure. He currently plays keyboard in Atlanta based dark ambient/noise/drone trio, Ibofanga. He lives in Mableton, GA.

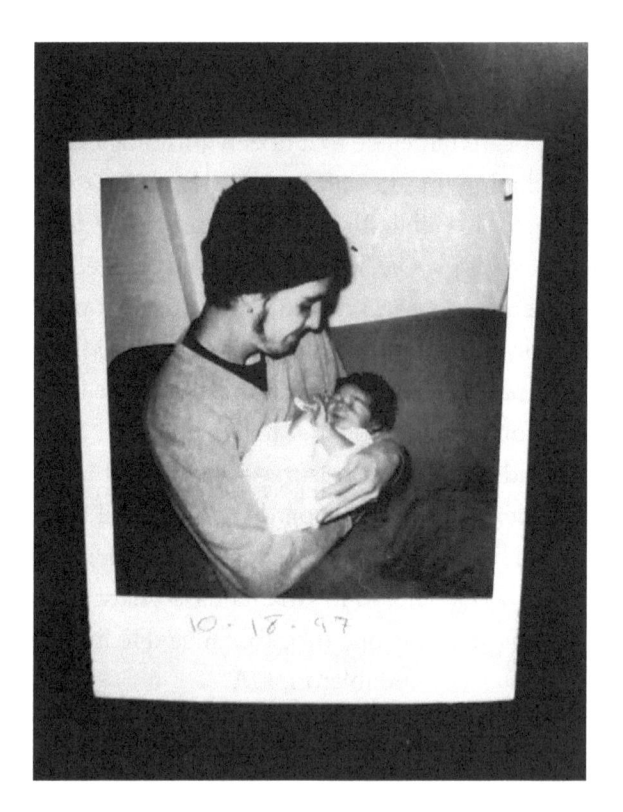

Author and son. Fall, 1997.

Made in United States
Troutdale, OR
12/03/2024

25656711R00148